MW00855804

LGBTQIA+ Books
for Children and Teens

ALA Editions purchases fund advocacy, awareness, and accreditation programs for library professionals worldwide.

SECOND EDITION

LGBTQIA+ BOOKS for Children and Teens

KATHLEEN BREITENBACH and LIZ DESKINS

ALA Editions

CHICAGO | 2023

© 2023 by Kathleen Breitenbach and Liz Deskins

Extensive effort has gone into ensuring the reliability of the information in this book; however, the publisher makes no warranty, express or implied, with respect to the material contained herein.

ISBN: 978-0-8389-3857-7 (paper)

Library of Congress Cataloging-in-Publication Data
Names: Breitenbach, Kathleen, author. | Deskins, Liz, author. | Dorr, Christina H. LGBTQAI+ books for children and teens.
Title: LGBTQIA+ books for children and teens / Kathleen Breitenbach and Liz Deskins.
Other titles: LGBTQIA plus books for children and teens
Description: Second edition / Kathleen Breitenbach and Liz Deskins. | Chicago : ALA Editions, 2023. | Includes bibliographical references and index. | Summary: "This resource discusses the best titles in LGBTQIA+ literature for children and teens and offers guidance on how to share this literature in ways that encourage understanding and acceptance among parents, administrators, and the wider community"—Provided by publisher.
Identifiers: LCCN 2022057355 | ISBN 9780838938577 (paperback)
Subjects: LCSH: Sexual minorities—Juvenile literature—Bibliography. | Sexual minorities in literature—Bibliography. | Children's literature—Study and teaching. | Young adult literature—Study and teaching. | Children—Books and reading—United States. | Teenagers—Books and reading—United States. | Sexual minority youth—Books and reading—United States. | Libraries—Special collections—Sexual minorities.
Classification: LCC Z7164.H74 D67 2023 HQ73 | DDC 028.70866—dc23/eng/20221212
LC record available at https://lccn.loc.gov/2022057355

Book design by Alejandra Diaz in the Questa, Effra and Phoreus Cherokee typefaces.

♾ This paper meets the requirements of ANSI/NISO Z39.48-1992 (Permanence of Paper).

Printed in the United States of America
27 26 25 24 23   5 4 3 2 1

CONTENTS

ACKNOWLEDGMENTS

The authors would like to acknowledge the help and support of the following groups and individuals: the ALA Editions team, especially Jamie Santoro; the Rainbow Round Table; the Rainbow Book List and Stonewall Youth Award committees; our families; the contributors who added fabulous annotations and ideas; and, of course, the authors who have given us these books to share with the world of children and young adult literature.

KB would also like to thank the staff of the RWJ Babs Siperstein Proud Center, especially Dr. Sam, Ashley, Aminah, and Jamila. Thanks also to my family, biological, created, and found. Allan: I hope you're proud of me.

LD would like to thank Bob and Brett for their inspiration and Allison Dorr for being a shining star. And most important, to Dr. Christina Dorr, my friend, my writing partner, and my partner in crime—thank you for always answering my call!

INTRODUCTION

How Can I Support My LGBTQIA+ Population Today?

A re you feeling overwhelmed trying to pick out diverse books for your collection? Are you worried about the rise in book challenges, especially against books with LGBTQIA+ topics, themes, and characters? Are you having trouble figuring out which books have different types of representation? If so, then congratulations, because you've come to the right place—those are exactly the types of problems this book aims to solve.

In this book, we are giving you the information you need to make your selections. Each book entry contains the complete title, author and illustrator, publisher, and date of publication, plus a note on what type(s) of LGBTQIA+ representation the book contains (see Decoding the Alphabet on page xi). Each book annotation shares what the book is about, and Conversation Starters provide opportunities to discuss the book. We show you where to find positive reviews of the book, with journal designations for starred titles. We also have responses from authors that explain not only why they write for children but what they feel teachers and librarians should understand when working with queer children and their classmates.

The book's six chapters follow the age range of readers:

- **Chapter 1,** "Ch-ch-changes!," covers some of the current crisis in book challenges and bans, how books for LGBTQIA+ readers are affected, and the effect such measures have.
- **Chapter 2,** "Books and Conversation for Young Readers," deals with a child's sense of self in their family and their larger community. It presents picture books that show all kinds of families, including those with parents and children who are not considered gender normative by conservative communities.

- **Chapter 3,** "Books and Conversations for Middle Grade Readers," focuses on books with young people who are questioning and finding themselves while searching for where they belong. It includes chapter books of varying lengths and with characters who are dealing with all the changes of middle school.
- **Chapter 4,** "Books and Conversation for Younger Teens," shares books that touch on mental health and other issues that develop as youth start high school.
- **Chapter 5,** "Books and Conversations for Older Teens," shares books that touch on housing insecurity and other issues that impact older teens.
- **Chapter 6,** "What Teachers and Librarians Can Do to Support LGBTQIA+ Students," shares action steps and best practices, as well as things that you can do in and for your community.

In this second edition, we focus mostly on current publications, from 2020 to 2023, because so many wonderful and worthy LGBTQIA+ books have been published in the past four years. A few from the first edition are still included; for example, *Heather Has Two Mommies*, which has had two editions so far. It was a groundbreaking book when it was first published and is still relevant, and challenged, today. When discussing touchstone books that helped to pave the way for today's LGBTQIA+ literature, we mention several classics but do not list or annotate them in the appropriate chapters. (Some of these are out of print but may be available at your library.)

EMERGING AND CHANGING TERMS

So much has changed in our vocabulary over the past few years, including the transition from using the acronym GLBT to using LGBTQIA+. The more accepted the community becomes, the greater the diversity in terminology, as people are able to be more open about and share their differences. This has resulted in more specific definitions, as we move from simply using the terms *gay* or *straight* to *gay/lesbian* to *gender identity* and *sexual orientation* and more; each term is acceptable and distinct. Instead of being overwhelming, this variety in terminology is our opportunity to allow for diversity in and individualization of gender identity. As you read through

DECODING THE ALPHABET

We abbreviate LGBTQIA+ representation types using the following definitions. When multiple identities are represented, we try to note the most prevalent representation first.

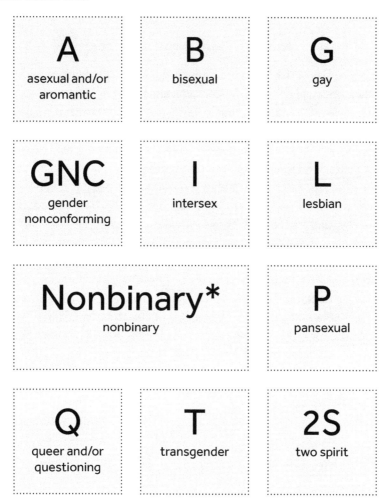

A asexual and/or aromantic	**B** bisexual	**G** gay
GNC gender nonconforming	**I** intersex	**L** lesbian
Nonbinary* nonbinary		**P** pansexual
Q queer and/or questioning	**T** transgender	**2S** two spirit

*This one is not abbreviated because *NB* is already used by others to signify "non-Black" when referring to people of color.

this book's chapters and annotations, know that we explain these terms, and more, in the glossary. Because language is fluid, these terms may change, and we are sensitive to that; we are choosing to be as inclusive as possible.

|||||||||||||||||||||||

Author/Contributor Biases

Readers may notice that we have not necessarily included all expected titles; because this volume contains annotations for our selected titles, we are limited to what books we and our contributors have read. Additionally, some representation categories may be larger or smaller than the percentage of books one might expect to see in that category; again, title selection is based on what we have read. For example, Kathleen is a teen librarian who is asexual and nonbinary and so will more often choose to read titles in those categories (teen/young adult books, books with asexual characters, books with nonbinary characters). This does not mean that those are the only books that Kathleen reads, but it does mean that Kathleen most likely reads a higher percentage of books that have asexual characters than they do books with characters of other sexualities. Liz is a retired school librarian and adjunct instructor of literature for children. She is a cisgender ally. Her choices of books to review are picture books and middle grade titles.

Ch-ch-changes!

More LGBTQIA+ books for children and young people are getting written and published, and more are coming from authentic voices. They continue to evolve and show a broader spectrum of LGBTQIA+ characters, both primary and secondary, and they all reveal the depth and variety of people and families today. That is the good news. The bad news is that book challenges have risen exponentially, especially for titles that represent the LGBTQIA+ community. Yet despite these threats, it is more important than ever to build collections that include these books. Librarians, teachers, and other professionals who work with children and young adults need to provide open discussions about these titles. Our spaces should be safe, warm, and welcoming for all children.

WHAT CHILDREN NEED

"It's incredibly important for an LGBTQ student who is being bullied in school and doesn't have support from their family to see that there are people in the world who are also LGBTQ and are thriving," says Alice O'Brien, general counsel for the National Education Association. "It's lifesaving for them. And the same is true for students of color. They need to see their experiences validated and reflected in the school curriculum and in our school library."[1]

COMING OUT IN THE PAGES: HISTORY OF LGBTQIA+ CHILDREN AND YOUNG ADULT LITERATURE

Today, we are finding quality picture books written about a variety of family structures with which all children can identify. Books for young adults have taken a similar path, one just as bumpy, with many challenges and issues. Even before we had literature classified as YA (young adult), there was a novel, *Chocolates for Breakfast* by Pamela Moore, first published in 1956, whose thirteen-year-old main character had a crush on her female teacher and a relationship with a bisexual man. This eye-opening book dealt frankly with issues about questioning one's sexual identity during the coming-of-age years.

Here are other examples of published books that offered windows and mirrors for children and young adults in the early 2000s. All have been challenged.

Rainbow Boys, written by Alex Sanchez and published in 2001, is the first in a series of books about high school boys who are frankly facing their homosexuality and everything that goes with it. AIDS, gay bashing, homophobia, and other topics are explored in this realistic fiction title.

Boy Meets Boy, written by David Levithan and published in 2003, called by some a "gay utopia," is the story of what life would be like at a school where everyone is gay. There are normal teen issues, but no angst about being gay. This delightful story is a great way to show that we may all be different, but we are also the same.

King and King, written by Linda de Haan and illustrated by Stern Nijland, published in 2003, finds the prince uninterested in the potential brides his mother parades by, as he has a prince in mind.

Luna, written by Julie Anne Peters and published in 2004, was the first YA book about a transgender character. Although they were called Liam by day, the main character did not really come alive until nighttime when they became Luna, decked out in beautiful dresses and makeup. Deciding to share Luna with their family and friends comes about through a voyage of self-discovery.

And Tango Makes Three, written by Justin Richardson and Peter Parnell and illustrated by Henry Cole, published in 2005, is a new and different way to present gay parents based on a true event at a public zoo. Although this book was the most challenged from 2005 to 2009, it had a second printing in 2015.

Fun Home: A Family Tragicomic, written by Alison Bechdel and published in 2007, is a graphic memoir that details Bechdel's life from childhood through college. During this time, she navigates the twists and turns of realizing she is lesbian while being raised by her closeted gay father, who runs the town funeral home. This is a unique recipe for a story, especially a true one, and it is told through a graphic novel, which was turned into a Broadway show.

Two Boys Kissing, written by David Levithan and published in 2013, has characters sharing an extended same-sex kiss because they are trying to break the Guinness World Record. The book is also notable because the story includes a chorus. It shares a heartfelt perspective and even a brief history of homosexuality.

None of the Above, written by I. W. Gregorio and published in 2015, became the first YA book to deal directly with the issues surrounding intersex people. Written by a doctor who also writes fiction, this story deals with a popular high school girl who seems to have everything. After a problem with her boyfriend, she visits her gynecologist and learns that she is intersex. Woven into the story is factual information about intersex organizations and medical treatments for intersex issues.

IIIIIIIIIIIIIIIIIIIIII

Maia Kobabe on the Watershed Moment in LGBTQIA+ YA Literature

[A]s a teenager in the early 2000s, the librarians at my library would make those little bookmarks with suggested titles and put them in different sections of the library, including a whole bookmark with queer titles, that they would then leave in the teen section. And I remember finding one of those as a teenager, and thinking, "I'm going to read every single book on this list," and I believe that I probably did, because there was a lot less queer YA available in 2003. There was, like, *Annie on My Mind,* and there was *Boy Meets Boy,* and there was *Luna* by Julie Anne Peters.[2] . . . 2003 was kind of like this real watershed moment of queer YA, and after that moment, there were so many more available. I was in eighth grade that year, so I feel like I was perfectly placed to receive that watershed of queer books that were then being published. Especially, here's the thing, before then, there were queer teen books, but they were all sad, they all had these tragic endings, often the queer character died, or was disowned by their family, or just had something really bad happen to them, and after that moment, there [were] people writing happy, lighthearted, more whimsical queer YA, and I feasted on those books, any queer book I could find. —MAIA KOBABE[3]

DEALING WITH OBJECTIONS

We look to see ourselves reflected in books, and we gain empathy by reading about people who are different from us. Unfortunately, book challenges and bans continue to impact books with queer content at a heavy rate, and such challenges "can actively harm teens for whom queer books serve as mirrors," says Karis Rogerson, writing for *We Need Diverse Books*.[4]

Challenges to materials were made at an alarming rate in both 2021 and 2022. After a relatively steady few years, the Office for Intellectual Freedom at the American Library Association reported 729 challenges or bans in 2021 and 1,269 in 2022.[5] PEN America did a nine-month study, which they then extended to a full year, of bans in school libraries and classrooms and found similar results.[6] Figure 1.1 shows just how sudden and extreme the increase in bans and challenges to books has become.

FIGURE 1.1

Reported challenges by year, from the ALA Office for Intellectual Freedom

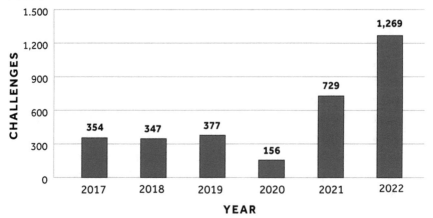

|||||||||||||||||||||||

Voices from the Stacks
Noah D. Mullens

I am a PhD student who studies LGBTQ+ Children's Literature. Before that (very before that), I grew up in a rural town with a small library that had no palpable queer presence. I did not identify as gay at the time, nor would I be allowed to engage with gay books. I felt a draw to certain novels over others to fill this void. These books, albeit trashy or flashy, gave me something that children's books did not. Put simply: I was the stereotype of the kid who read only "adult" novels (think V. C. Andrews or Stephen King).

Now flash forward. The kid who read adult novels is now the adult who reads children's literature. In my studies I find LGBTQ+ children's books that range from the rich and incredible to the narrow and didactic. Nevertheless, the essential trait of these books is that they are fruitful and that they multiply. Kids in libraries can roam the stacks and find new and exciting books that show something I thought was beyond belief.

Even so, it is risky to be too utopian; the accessibility of these books is under attack through "new" bans. But these books have always been under attack. The title of this book is proof that LGBTQ+ books are windows into the lives and experiences of people. I propose that they are also mirrors that remind us to never take progress for granted. That kid in a rural town still exists; it's just about finding a way to reach him.

Authorities challenging, banning, and burning books is not new. Historically, these bans and burns have been led by religious and governmental leaders. One need not look even a century in the past to consider the efforts of the German Nazi Party in looting and burning the contents of the Institute for Sexual Science in Berlin in 1933, or the government of South Africa banning anti-apartheid materials from the 1950s. Even more recently is Russia's "gay propaganda" law, banning any information on LGBTQIA+ topics, which was signed in 2013.

In the United States, books have been challenged, for various reasons, since before it was even a country.[7] Recently, though, challenges and bans have been escalating. According to *Banned in the USA,* PEN America's Index of School Book Bans "highlighted the disproportionate targeting of books by or about people whose identities and stories have traditionally been underrepresented in children's and young adult literature, such as people of color, LGBTQ+ individuals, or persons with disabilities."[8] They looked at book bans only in school libraries and classrooms in the United States and only within a nine-month span (July 1, 2021 to March 31, 2022). Despite the short time frame, they index "1,586 instances of individual books being banned, affecting 1,145 unique book titles." Even worse,

> 41% (644 individual bans) are tied to directives from state officials or elected lawmakers to investigate or remove books in schools. . . . [B]ook banning, as a form of censorship, implicates First Amendment prohibitions on the ability of government entities to ban or punish expression, making these documented efforts by lawmakers all the more concerning.[9]

Maia Kobabe, author of *Gender Queer,* which has been the subject of numerous challenges, bans, and an attempted lawsuit in Virginia, makes stark the connections between book challenges and bills restricting rights for LGBTQIA+ people:

> I think it is a very organized effort to erase trans and queer and non-binary voices from the public sphere. And I see it as linked to also the rise in bills trying to limit access to trans healthcare, and limit the rights of trans athletes and trans students to access various activities and sports in school. I see it as a very dangerous and upsetting effort to make it harder for trans people and nonbinary and queer people to live.[10]

Of particular note for this volume, the PEN America Index notes that in the full yearlong look that they took at book challenges and bans in classrooms and school libraries, they found "2,532 instances of individual books being banned, affecting 1,648 unique book titles,"[11] with 674 (41 percent) titles that include LGBTQ+ themes or characters. Of the 262 titles we include in this edition, 92 (35 percent) have been targeted in those bans. The top two titles on their list, *Gender Queer* by Maia Kobabe (challenged in forty-one districts) and *All Boys Aren't Blue* by George M. Johnson (challenged in twenty-nine districts), are included in this edition, and of their top nineteen titles, eight have LGBTQIA+ content (42 percent). Looking at their list of the top forty-six banned authors for this period, we include at least one book by twelve of them (26 percent).

The Office for Intellectual Freedom at the American Library Association notes similar troubling cases. After a large dip in 2020 due to schools and libraries being mostly closed due to the COVID-19 pandemic, book challenges and bans surged by more than 360 percent (see figure 1.1), and titles impacted increased by almost 500 percent, as shown starkly in figure 1.2. Of note,

> half of the American Library Association's top 10 list of most challenged books in 2021 concern queer identity, and the three most challenged books—*Gender Queer: A Memoir* by Maia Kobabe, *Lawn Boy* by Jonathan Evison, and *All Boys Aren't Blue* by George M. Johnson—all fall in this category.[12]

FIGURE 1.2

Reported titles challenged by year, from the ALA Office for Intellectual Freedom

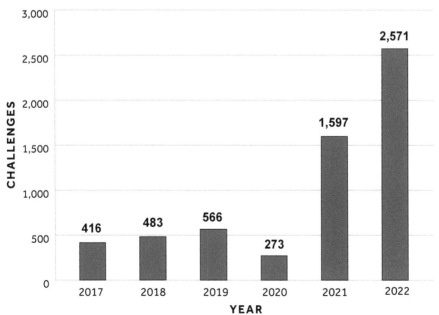

||||||||||||||||||||||||

Authors Speak Out on Book Bans

"Removing or restricting queer books in libraries and schools is like cutting a lifeline for queer youth, who might not yet even know what terms to ask Google to find out more about their own identities, bodies and health."—**MAIA KOBABE**[13]

"Hiding the beautiful range of humanity from young people does not keep young people from being themselves. Instead, it makes the road for queer and trans people to find ourselves harder and more damaging, and leaves a large majority of cisgender people who don't know us, and therefore are much more likely to read, and hurt us. Positive representation saves lives."—**ALEX GINO**[14]

"Kids are the same everywhere. There are depressed kids everywhere. There are isolated, at-risk kids everywhere. There are LGBTQ kids everywhere. Getting rid of books from the library won't change that; it will just make life that much harder and more isolated for those children. . . . The truth is that like it or not, some kids are gay. Some kids are trans. To make the world safer and better for them, we need to have representation of those people in books. Books with LGBTQ characters save lives. I know because of the hundreds of emails I've received from kids who have told me my books saved their life."—**BILL KONIGSBERG**[15]

"We have an issue in this country, specifically when it comes to young adults, that we assume that there are topics that are too heavy for them to read or to understand. I am not a believer of that. . . . There is this belief that if we keep these things away from the youth, that they won't indulge in them, when the reality is [that] us keeping resources, and us keeping these stories, away from them doesn't stop them from going through the same situations. It just means that they don't have the knowledge or the education to handle those situations in a way that can be best suited for them."—**GEORGE M. JOHNSON**[16]

Though more common in the past, children are still often discouraged by well-meaning adults and other professionals from discussing family situations and their own gender identities. Every child deserves to feel represented, valued, understood, and welcomed. Without these books, we lose the opportunity to explore and understand these issues in ways that will build empathy. These books are written to examine the issues of understanding, empathy, acceptance, and respecting inherent human rights. They are written not only so that LGBTQIA+ youth do not feel invisible or of less value but also so that straight, cisgender youth can feel empathy and gain an understanding of their classmates and friends.

So if we agree all children need exposure to LGBTQIA+ books and honest, open discussion, how do we deal with stakeholders who disagree? Begin by taking a look at your collection, library, or classroom, and ask the following questions:

- Do you have a variety of fiction and nonfiction titles that explore LGBTQIA+ themes?
- Do you have titles with diverse secondary characters that offer a realistic mix of people one might expect to find in a group?
- Are there titles written on a variety of reading and interest levels?
- If they are genrefied, are these books blended in with their genres or do you have a separate section?

Though there's validity to both approaches, we'd argue that unless you separate out books with topics related to other forms of diversity (race, ethnicity, class, age, etc.), then don't form a separate section for LGBTQIA+ books.

Why share LGBTQIA+ literature with all children? Because, we argue, it's an issue of fundamental rights—rights that all of us deserve. We no longer hesitate to share books about other forms of diversity: race, ethnicity, socioeconomic status, age, language, women's issues, and more. Why are we still hesitant to share books about sexual orientation, gender identity and expression, and nontraditional family structures with all children?

||||||||||||||||||||||||

Authors Speak Up for Book Inclusion

Arguments for the inclusion of these books in libraries and curricula for all children come from a wide variety of sources. Gene Luen Yang, author of the Printz Award–winning young adult graphic novel *American Born Chinese* and the fifth National Ambassador for Young People's Literature named by the Library of Congress, had this to say at a conference a few years ago: "Books themselves are ambassadors . . . books can be advocates. . . . This is why we need diverse books [as they] teach kids to love others [and act as a] moral foundation."[17]

Books can be good advocates, but they can also be actively harmful if they portray a negative or stereotypical view of LGBTQIA+ children. Rudine Sims Bishop, an enduring voice in the field of diverse children's literature, writes:

> When children cannot find themselves reflected in the books they read, or when the images they see are distorted, negative, or laughable, they learn a powerful lesson about how they are devalued in the society of which they are a part.[18]

This makes it even more important for books that reinforce a positive, valuable image for children and young people to be readily available and accessible. Characters like Julián (*Julián Is a Mermaid*), Max (*Call Me Max*), and Violet (*Love, Violet*) can show that being different and proud of oneself is wonderful.

> Therefore, accurate and inclusive portrayals of LGBTQ individuals in picture books serve as positive role models with whom LGBTQ children can connect . . . , letting them know they are not alone, and provides them with a broader understanding of themselves (mirror) and others (window).[19]

WHERE LIBRARIANS FIT IN

Librarians—school, public, and all other types—still face the stereotypes of being old fashioned, out of date, and nonprofessional, when nothing could be further from the truth. We're truly a strong group of professionals who take our patrons' needs and interests to heart and are willing to fight for them and their rights. We hope the tools we include in this book will further your resolve to ask the questions that help promote understanding and empathy about LGBTQIA+ issues with all children at a time when it's crucially needed.

Banning and challenging books does not impact only readers whose identities are reflected in the books being banned. PEN America notes,

> The move to ban both fiction and non-fiction books dealing with diverse characters and experiences—including racial, ethnic, and religious identities; gender identities and sexual orientations—reflects a backlash against attempts to bring a more diverse and inclusive set of voices and perspectives into the curriculum. This impacts students with these identities who may feel excluded; but also the opportunity for all students to learn about differences.[20]

Rogerson quotes Lee-Ann Gill, a teen librarian:

> The book challenges and the book banning—what it says to the teens, who may identify with those books, [is] that they are banned. That they should be challenged, not allowed to be who they are. Not able to be themselves. [That] it's not normal, it's not okay.[21]

And Erika Long, a library consultant in Tennessee says, "It's part of the teen experience, or adolescent experience, to experience a kiss. But that doesn't make it obscene just because it involves two boys or two girls."[22]

And maybe most simply and directly put by author Kelly Barnhill, "If you change the narrative, you change the world."[23] So, let's all take the prickly path and begin to change the world.

NOTES

1. Quoted in Sarah Wood, "Book Bans: What to Know," *US News and World Report,* May 17, 2022, under "Impact of Book Bans," www.usnews.com/education/k12/articles/book-bans-what-to-know.
2. As noted earlier, *Luna* was published in 2004.
3. Maia Kobabe, "Maia Kobabe—Gender Queer—at Conn Ave with Kathleen Breitenbach" (author talk, Politics and Prose Bookstore, Washington, D.C., June 26, 2022).

4. Karis Rogerson, "How LGBTQIA+ Book Bans Impact Kids and Teens," *We Need Diverse Books* (blog), March 25, 2022, para. 6, https://diversebooks.org/how-lgbtqia-book-bans-impact-kids-and-teens/.

5. "Censorship by the Numbers," Office for Intellectual Freedom (American Library Association), www.ala.org/advocacy/sites/ala.org.advocacy/files/content/banned/bannedbooksweek/BBW22-bythenumbers-fullpage.pdf; American Library Association, "American Library Association Reports Record Number of Demands to Censor Library Books and Materials in 2022," news release, March 22, 2023.

6. Jonathan Friedman and Nadine Farid Johnson, *Banned in the USA: The Growing Movement to Censor Books in Schools* (PEN America, September 19, 2022), https://pen.org/report/banned-usa-growing-movement-to-censor-books-in-schools/.

7. Ally Bush, "The Little-Known History of Banned Books in the United States," *Reading Partners* (blog), March 3, 2021, https://readingpartners.org/blog/history-banned-books-week/.

8. Johnathan Friedman and Nadine Farid Johnson, *Banned in the USA: Rising School Book Bans Threaten Free Expression and Students' First Amendment Rights (April 2022)* (PEN America, September 14, 2022), para. 2, https://pen.org/banned-in-the-usa/.

9. Friedman and Johnson, *Banned in the USA: Rising School Book Bans*, under "Alarming Trends."

10. Madeleine Carlisle, "'Gender Queer' Author on Efforts to Ban Book, Virginia Suit," *Time*, August 31, 2022, under question 6, https://time.com/6210087/gender-queer-book-ban-maia-kobabe/.

11. Friedman and Johnson, *Banned in the USA: Growing Movement to Censor,* under "Banned Book Data Snapshot."

12. Marva Hinton, "You've Got a Friend in Me," *School Library Journal,* June 2022, 27.

13. Maia Kobabe, "Schools Are Banning My Book, but Queer Kids Need Queer Stories," *Washington Post,* November 11, 2021, para. 8, www.washingtonpost.com/opinions/2021/10/29/schools-are-banning-my-book-queer-kids-need-queer-stories/.

14. Quoted in Friedman and Johnson, *Banned in the USA: Rising School Book Bans,* under "What Stories Are Being Banned?"

15. Bill Konigsberg, "An Open Letter to Parents Who Wish to Ban My Books from School Libraries," Bill Konigsberg, February 20, 2022, para. 14 and para. 19, https://billkonigsberg.com/an-open-letter-to-parents-who-wish-to-ban-my-books-from-school-libraries/.

16. Quoted in Friedman and Johnson, *Banned in the USA: Rising School Book Bans,* under "What Is a School Book Ban?"

17. Gene Luen Yang, untitled (address, Pickerington Teen Book Fest [PTBF], Pickerington, OH, June 11, 2016).

18. "Rudine Sims Bishop," Tumblr, accessed August 2022, www.tumblr.com/search/rudine sims bishop. This quote is from her book *Free Within Ourselves: The Development of African American Children's Literature* (Heinemann, 2007).

19. Enoch Leung and Julia Adams-Whittaker, "Content Analysis of LGBTQ Picture Books for Elementary Education through an Intersectional Lens," *Frontiers in Education* 25 (January 2022), "Introduction," para. 3, https://doi.org/10.3389/feduc.2021.769769.

20. Friedman and Johnson, *Banned in the USA: Rising School Book Bans,* under "What Stories Are Being Banned?"

21. Quoted in Rogerson, "How LGBTQIA+ Book Bans Impact Kids and Teens," para. 7.

22. Hinton, "You've Got a Friend in Me," 28.

23. Kelly Barnhill, untitled (address, *School Library Journal* Day of Dialog, Chicago, IL, May 11, 2016).

Books and Conversation for Young Readers

Because we know the magical feeling we get when we hear a new book, we understand the joy of sharing a book with our young readers and listening to them discuss what they enjoyed and discovered. Using high-quality picture books, we can introduce the variety of people, genders, colors, languages, and belief systems in our world. Dr. Rudine Sims Bishop wrote that books can be

> windows into the realities of others, not just imaginary worlds, and books can be mirrors that reflect the lives of readers. Sliding glass doors refers to how readers can walk into a story and become part of the world created by the author—readers become fully immersed in another experience.[1]

Approaching children's stories through the lens of windows, mirrors, and sliding glass doors prioritizes diversity, honors many cultures, and promotes empathy. Too often, missing from these opportunities are inclusive families, same-sex couples, trans parents, and, most important, transgender, nonbinary, and gender-nonconforming children. Overwhelmingly, queer picture books feature queer adults or are about general queer topics, but we're starting to see more books featuring kids exploring gender or expressing attraction for another kid of the same gender.

||||||||||||||||||||||

Start Small
The First Picture Books to Add to Your Collection

- *What Are Your Words? A Book about Pronouns* by Katherine Locke
- *Cinderelliot: A Scrumptious Fairytale* by Mark Ceilley and Rachel Smoka-Richardson
- *The Name I Call Myself* by Cathryn John and Hasan Namir

WHAT YOUNG CHILDREN NEED

We believe that picture books are an integral part of a child's learning of the world around them, beginning with their family, then larger family structure, the classroom, and, finally, the larger community around them. Because of this, it is important to have high-quality picture books that show the power of family. All kinds of families—two moms, two dads, one mom, grandparents as caregivers, and any others—should be modeled in these books. Picture books show a child the diversity in families they may not experience, from who makes up a family to what they do as various family traditions.[2] Beyond modeling a myriad of family makers, picture books show family traditions of these families, which is beneficial to all children.

SPECIAL FOCUS: DIVERSE FAMILIES

There are many reasons to share books that demonstrate diverse families, but the most important is this: children are naturally curious. They ask questions, a lot of them, and having picture books that can address these questions is an easy and accessible way to handle them. Additionally, but of no less importance, having these books shared in a classroom helps each child feel like their family may be different from their classmates' but still equal in terms of acceptance. According to Erica Long, a middle school librarian in Tennessee, "A good book can help you understand what it's like for people who don't share your race, religion, sexual orientation, or socio-economic status. Diverse books teach empathy."[3]

IIIIIIIIIIIIIIIIIIIII

Voices from the Stacks
Ariana Hussain

As a teacher-librarian in an elementary school setting, having LGBTQIA+ youth lit on our library shelves, in our classroom, and in our curriculum enables us to foster a more inclusive community at school and beyond. Our lower school library collection mostly includes books that reflect inclusive family structures as well as gender identity and expression, but also attraction. The palpable joy of students who have physically embraced a book with a nonbinary character, or have been told that they don't need to whisper when asking for books with two girls in love, is something that is powerful but is also coupled with extreme guilt on my part. Because I know that being in an independent school, whose core values include affirming the identity of all of our students, means that we can often protect our Queer students (and sometimes their families and our staff) from the vitriol that is being spewed in many of our public institutions, be they schools or public libraries, that are the focus of challenges of books featuring Queer, Black, Indigenous, people of color voices, characters, and experiences. Recognizing and affirming identity as a core community value also means that my Queer colleagues, my other colleagues of color, my other Muslim colleagues, and myself are better able to bring our full selves to school every day. It's not perfect, and of course there are obstacles, resistance, and growth at frustratingly incremental levels at times. But it makes me feel a sense of physical, mental, and emotional safety that we recognize inequity, that our struggles are interconnected, and that collectively we are willing and moving toward a community where all are welcome and cherished.

TRENDS IN LGBTQIA+ PICTURE BOOKS

Lesléa Newman is the author of more than fifty books, including *Heather Has Two Mommies,* the first children's book to portray lesbian families in a positive way. On her website she says,

Many years ago, a woman stopped me on the street and said, "I don't have a book to read to my daughter that shows a family like ours. Someone should write one." So I did! I hope *Heather Has Two Mommies* shows that there are many types of families in the world, and the most important thing about any family is that it is filled with love.[4]

‖‖‖‖‖‖‖‖‖‖‖‖‖‖‖‖‖‖

Authors Speak Out
Lesléa Newman

I think it's important to understand that LGBTQ+ kids need a lot of support. They may or may not have support at home, they may or may not have support from peers, and it's important to just assume that there are LGBTQ+ kids, or kids with parents or siblings or grandparents or friends [who are LGBTQ+], in your classroom. Don't wait until it's obvious that you have [such] a student to give that information to everybody. Everybody needs to learn to accept, respect, and celebrate the entire diverse spectrum of our human experience.

We are fortunate to have quality picture books that show the many types of families, people, and children that young readers will encounter in real life. There are many wonderful books from which to choose, and we love sharing them with you.

As you can see from figure 2.1, the number of LGBTQIA+ picture books that were selected for the Rainbow Book List has been increasing. However, figure 2.2 reveals that there are still small groups of the LGBTQIA+ community who are underrepresented, so there is still work to do. The Rainbow Round Table (RRT), part of the American Library Association (ALA) and creator of the Rainbow Book List, "is committed to serving the information needs of the LGBTQIA+ professional library community, and the LGBTQIA+ information and access needs of individuals at large."[5] It is also committed to encouraging and supporting free and necessary access to all information, in line with ALA's mission.

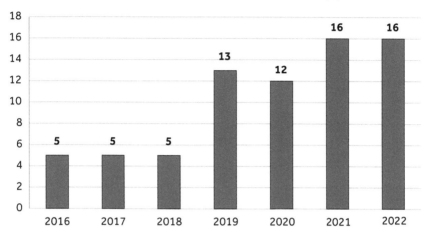

FIGURE 2.1

Number of picture books on the Rainbow Book List by year

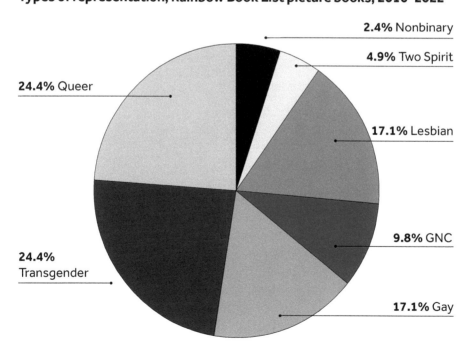

FIGURE 2.2

Types of representation, Rainbow Book List picture books, 2016–2022*

*In this figure, percentages have been rounded to the nearest tenth.

PICTURE BOOKS THAT CAN BE USED IN OTHER DISPLAYS

Black History Month
Calvin   My Sister Daisy
My Rainbow   When Aidan Became a Brother

Hispanic Heritage Month
Julián Is a Mermaid

Asian American and Pacific Islander Month
Ho'onani: Hula Warrior

Valentine's Day/Romance
Love, Violet

Native American Heritage Month
47,000 Beads   Sharice's Big Voice: A Native Kid
                                        Becomes a Congresswoman

Summer
The Meaning of Pride   The Rainbow Parade
Pride Puppy!   'Twas the Night before Pride

Autism Acceptance Month
My Rainbow

PICTURE BOOK FICTION

***Big Wig* by Jonathan Hillman, illustrated by Levi Hastings. Paula Wiseman Books, 2022. (GNC)**

A wig travels with a child to a Big Wig Ball for drag queens young and old but starts to feel small next to the much bigger wigs of the other queens. When a gust of wind blows Wig around, landing on head after head, Wig starts to grow bigger with everyone's confidence. Eventually, Wig lands back on her friend's head.

Conversation Starters
1. What gives you confidence?
2. Is there something you carry for confidence? What is it?

Call Me Max by Kyle Lukoff, illustrated by Luciano Lozano. Reycraft Books, 2019. (T)

Because Max's parents and teacher don't know that he's a boy, it takes bravery to speak up and tell them that he's transgender.

Conversation Starters
1. What kind of person do you feel like on the inside?
2. What kind of friend would you be to a boy like this?

Calvin by J. R. Ford and Vanessa Ford, illustrated by Kayla Harren. G. P. Putnam's Sons Books for Young Readers, 2021. (T)

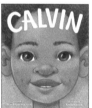

When Calvin finally tells his family that he's a boy, and not a girl like they'd thought, he's met with support, as well as a trip for new swim trunks and a new haircut for his first day of school.

Awards and Honors
- Starred review: *Booklist*
- Lambda Literary Award for LGBTQ Children's/Middle Grade, 2022
- Rainbow Book List Top Ten for Young Readers, 2022

Conversation Starters
1. What scares you about starting school?
2. How do you share changes in your life with others?

Cinderelliot: A Scrumptious Fairytale by Mark Ceilley and Rachel Smoka-Richardson, illustrated by Stephanie Laberis. Running Press Kids, 2022. (G)

In this retelling of Cinderella, Cinder is a boy who bakes, which was the one thing his stepsister and stepbrother liked about him. One day, the prince hosts an event asking citizens to bring their best baked item and the winner would become the royal baker. After baking items for his stepsiblings to take, Cinderelliot cleans the kitchen, wishing he could attend with his favorite chocolate cake. Suddenly, his fairy godfather appears! With a flick of a wand, Cinderelliot has everything he needs to bake his cake. Then with a swish of the wand, his fairy godfather cleans the kitchen and dresses Cinderelliot in a handsome baker's uniform with a white chef's hat. When he reaches the prince, sparks and sprinkles fly, and Cinderelliot becomes the prince's baker!

Awards and Honors
- Rainbow Book List, 2023

Conversation Starters
1. What things are different in this story compared to the regular Cinderella?
2. What kind of Cinderella story would you write?

Dolls and Trucks Are for Everyone by Robb Pearlman, illustrated by Eda Kaban. Running Press Kids, 2021. (Q)

This simple picture book reinforces the message that toys are for every kid, "girls, boys, and everyone."

Conversation Starters
1. What do you use to create things?
2. Are robots for puppies? Why or why not?

47,000 Beads by Koja Adeyoha and Angel Adeyoha, illustrated by Holly McGillis. Flamingo Rampant, 2017. (2S)

Peyton loves to dance powwow but feels constrained by jingle dancing. Luckily, Auntie Eyota knows just what to do and asks Grandparent L and the rest of the community for help.

Conversation Starters
1. Do you know what *two spirit* means?
2. Does your culture have traditions and special events?

Grandad's Camper by Harry Woodgate. Little Bee Books, 2021. (G)

A young child visits her Grandad's house in the summer, and the two reminisce about the child's Gramps, who has passed away, and all of the adventures Grandad and Gramps went on. Soon the child and Grandad are fixing up the camper van and setting off on adventures of their own.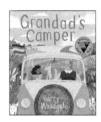

Awards and Honors
- Starred reviews: *Kirkus Reviews, School Library Journal*
- Stonewall Honor Book in Children's Literature, 2022
- Waterstones Children's Book Prize for Best Illustrated Book, 2022

Conversation Starters
1. Where do you like to travel?
2. What fun times can you think of that you shared with an older person in your life?
3. What is your favorite adventure place to visit?

Heather Has Two Mommies by Lesléa Newman, illustrated by Laura Cornell. Candlewick Press, 2015. (L, G)

This quiet but groundbreaking story is a classic in LGBTQIA+ children's books. First written in 1979, republished in 1989 and again in 2015 with new illustrations, this story of two women wanting to create a family is still relevant today. Kate and Jane decide to use in vitro fertilization, and Heather is born. When she enters preschool, she discovers the wide array of family structures in which her classmates live. She's part of a loving family and an accepting world beyond. The soft-pencil sketches and simple but matter-of-fact writing clearly tell the story of Heather's beginning, birth, and growth with honesty and joy.

Conversation Starters
1. How does Heather feel about her mommies?
2. How are the families of her friends different from hers? How do they feel about their families?

||||||||||||||||||||||

Ask an Author with Lesléa Newman

Q: How did growing up in the LBGTQIA+ community, or lack of community, mold your ideas for your writing?

I did not grow up in an LGBTQ+ community. I came out when I was twenty-seven and before that I really didn't have any awareness—though when I look back, I see, and have since learned, that one of my high school teachers was a lesbian. I didn't know until I was probably in my forties and reconnected with her. The only out gay person that I knew I met when I was twenty-five, and that was my mentor Allen Ginsberg, when I studied poetry at the Jack Kerouac School of Disembodied Poetics at the Europa Institute. If I had grown up in an LGBTQ+ community, or even just knew that it existed, I would have come out earlier and I would have written about the issues that are important to the LGBTQ+ community earlier.

Q: In this socially and politically divisive time in our country, what message would you like your books to share?

What I have always tried to do in my books, and it hasn't changed, is give a message that all children are accepted, respected, and celebrated. So I would like every child to walk away feeling like there's a place for me and I belong.

Ho'onani: Hula Warrior **by Heather Gale, illustrated by Mika Song. Tundra Books, 2019. (2S)**

Ho'onani loves hula, but she doesn't feel like a girl or a boy. She's somewhere in the middle. When her school performs a traditional kane hula chant, can she find a way to lead the all-male troupe? This book is based on real events with real people.

Awards and Honors
- Starred review: *Publishers Weekly*

Conversation Starters
1. What are ways that you feel different from other kids?
2. Do you ever have to work at making space to belong?

If You're a Drag Queen and You Know It by Lil Miss Hot Mess, illustrated by Olga de Dios. Running Press Kids, 2022. (GNC)

Perfect for storytime (especially drag queen storytime), this picture book is a fabulous, drag queen–ified version of "If You're Happy and You Know It." Kids can wink, twirl, and say "Yesss, Queen" along with the song/story.

Conversation Starters
1. Can you show me your twirls?
2. What do you like about the illustrations?

Julián Is a Mermaid by Jessica Love. Candlewick Press, 2018. (GNC)

Julián is a young boy on a trip with his abuela when they see mermaids on their train. He loves mermaids, and when they get home, he wraps himself in curtains and plants and declares that he, too, is a mermaid, before his abuela takes him to see the Coney Island Mermaid Parade.

Awards and Honors
- Starred reviews: *Bulletin of the Center for Children's Books, Horn Book, Kirkus Reviews, Publishers Weekly, School Library Journal*
- NAIBA Books of the Year Award for Picture Book, 2018
- Goodreads Choice Award, Picture Books nominee, 2018
- Stonewall Book Award–Mike Morgan and Larry Romans Children's Literature Award, 2019
- Jane Addams Children's Book Award Honor Book for Younger Children, 2019
- Ezra Jack Keats Book Award for Illustrator nominee, 2019

Conversation Starters
1. Is there anything that you like that you're scared someone will be mad at you for liking?
2. What do you like to dress up as?

||||||||||||||||||||||

Ask an Author with Jessica Love

Q: What is one thing you'd like librarians, teachers, and other community members working with LBGTQIA+ youth to understand?
[L]et people tell you who they are.

Love, Violet by Charlotte Sullivan Wild, illustrated by Charlene Chua. Farrar, Straus and Giroux Books for Young Readers, 2022. (L)

Violet is a little girl, but she has a large crush on someone in her class. She is too shy to tell her outgoing friend Mira how she feels, but for Valentine's Day she makes Mira a valentine and signs it "Love, Violet." Violet is too shy to give it to Mira, until a big gust of wind helps her out!

Awards and Honors
- Starred reviews: *Kirkus Reviews, Publishers Weekly*
- Stonewall Book Awards–Mike Morgan and Larry Romans Children's Literature Award, 2023
- Rainbow Book List, 2023

Conversation Starters
1. Have you ever been shy about giving a friend a gift? How did you handle it?
2. What is a different way Violet might have used to give Mira the valentine?

Mama and Mommy and Me in the Middle by Nina LaCour, illustrated by Kaylani Juanita. Candlewick, 2022. (L)

When Mama has to go on a work trip for a whole week, a young child struggles with missing her. But the child and Mommy talk about all the things they do because Mama's gone and how happy they'll be when she's home.

Awards and Honors
- Starred reviews: *Booklist, Publishers Weekly*
- Rainbow Book List Top Ten for Young Readers, 2023

Conversation Starters
1. Do you have special things you do with your parents/caregivers?
2. How do you feel when your parent/caregiver is away?

Me and My Dysphoria Monster by Laura Kate Dale, illustrated by Hui Qing Ang. Jessica Kingsley Publishers, 2022. (T)

Nisha has a monster, and it gets bigger when people call her a boy. When she meets another transgender person, though, she learns ways to make her monster smaller again.

Awards and Honors
• Rainbow Book List, 2023

Conversation Starters
1. What would your monster look like?
2. What makes your monster bigger or smaller?

The Meaning of Pride by Rosiee Thor, illustrated by Sam Kirk. Versify, 2022. (Q)

This vibrant book explores the history and significance of Pride parades and festivals.

Conversation Starters
1. How can you show pride?
2. What makes you proud?

Miss Rita, Mystery Reader by Sam Donovon and Kristen Wixted, illustrated by Violet Tobacco. Farrar, Straus and Giroux, 2022. (GNC)

Tori, a gender-nonconforming child, is excited that her father is the mystery reader in her classroom. Her dad is excited too. He is dressing up as Miss Rita, a drag queen. As Tori helps him get ready and chooses what wig and what dress Dad will wear, worries come. Will classroom friends like him? Will they understand his job? Will they like to hear him read a book? The sensitive father sees the worry and calms the fears. Miss Rita Book is a class mystery reader success!

Awards and Honors
- Starred review: *Booklist*
- Rainbow Book List, 2023

Conversation Starters
1. Who would you like as a mystery reader?
2. Do you like it when a parent visits your class? Why or why not?

My Moms Love Me by Anna Membrino, illustrated by Joy Hwang Ruiz. Orchard Books, 2022. (L)

In short, rhyming text, a baby narrates their day and all the ways their moms show how much they love them. The pastel illustrations are welcoming and the family faces are loving, just the way a baby knows they are loved.

Awards and Honors
- Rainbow Book List, 2023

Conversation Starters
1. What do your grown-ups do that show you they love you?
2. What do you do to show your grown-ups that you love them?

My Own Way: Celebrating Gender Freedom for Kids by Joana Estrela, adapted by Jay Hulme. Wide Eyed Editions, 2022. (T)

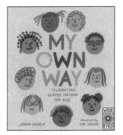

In rhyming text, this book shows children that there are many ways to be themselves.

Conversation Starters
1. Do you always like the things everyone expects you to like?
2. What is your own special thing?

My Rainbow by Trinity and DeShanna Neal, illustrated by Art Twink. Kokila, 2020. (T)

Trinity wants long hair, but none of the wigs at the beauty store are right, so Trinity's mom creates a beautiful rainbow wig.

Awards and Honors
- Starred reviews: *Kirkus Reviews, Publishers Weekly*

Conversation Starters
1. If you could make your hair look like anything you want, what would it look like? Can you draw a picture?
2. What suggestions do you have for Trinity and her hair?

My Shadow Is Purple by Scott Stuart. Larrikin House, 2022. (Nonbinary)

This simple, gentle rhyming story allows a child to understand that they are special and unique just as they are! Through the use of colored shadows, people are shown conforming to pink and blue. But our protagonist has a purple shadow and likes to do things that both pink and blue shadows do. Finally forced to choose a color, the child says, "I'll just go home," which gives other children the bravery to jump up and share their colors. No two are the same, and all are unique!

Conversation Starters
1. What kinds of things do you like to do? Do they make you happy?
2. Does it make a difference if you play with "boy" toys or "girl" toys?

My Sister Daisy by Adria Karlsson, illustrated by Linus Curci. Capstone, 2021. (T)

A boy has a younger sibling, and they love playing together as they grow. After kindergarten, though, the younger sibling lets her family know that she's a girl.

Conversation Starters

1. How would the brother continue to play with his sister? Would he need to share new games, or would they continue to play the games they both love?
2. In what ways can the brother support his younger sibling?

The Name I Call Myself by Hasan Namir, illustrated by Cathryn John. Arsenal Pulp Press, 2020. (Nonbinary)

Ari doesn't like the name their parents call them. As they grow up, we see them struggle with societal expectations and learn who they are.

Conversation Starters

1. Does your name feel like you?
2. How would you feel if someone told you that something you like "isn't for boys" or "isn't for girls"?

Patience, Patches! by Christy Mihaly, illustrated by Sheryl Murray. Dial Books for Young Readers, 2022. (L)

Patches is a happy dog with two moms. One feeds him, and the other plays with him. One day they leave and say, "We'll be back soon. Be patient." So Patches is patient and waits and waits. Finally, his moms come home, but they bring home a blanket bundle with them, and things have changed. This bundle takes up his moms' time, and they keep saying, "Patience, Patches." So Patches is patient, and finally the blanket bundle turns into something he can play with, a baby.

Awards and Honors

• Rainbow Book List, 2023

Conversation Starters

1. What does Patches like about his two moms?
2. Do you think you could have that much patience? What would you do while waiting?

Pride Colors by Robin Stevenson. Orca, 2019. (Q)

This board book not only falls under the genre of teaching colors to small children but also reinforces themes of inclusion, affirmation, and connection.

Awards and Honors
- Starred reviews: *Kirkus Reviews, School Library Journal*
- Lambda Literary Award for LGBTQ Children's/Young Adult finalist, 2020

Conversation Starters
1. What are your favorite colors?
2. Is there a picture that looks like you or your family?

Pride Puppy! by Robin Stevenson, illustrated by Julie McLaughlin. Orca Books, 2021. (Q)

The whole family goes to the Pride parade, and there's so much to do. Unfortunately, their dog gets lost at the parade! Luckily, there's a whole lot of people to help find the lost puppy.

Awards and Honors
- Starred reviews: *Kirkus Reviews, Publishers Weekly*

Conversation Starters
1. Do you have a pet? What kind?
2. What's your favorite type of animal?

The Rainbow Parade by Emily Neilson. Dial Books, 2022. (L, Q)

Emily and her moms go to a big parade in June. There's so much for them to see. When they ask if she wants to join the parade, Emily doesn't know what to do.

Awards and Honors
- Starred reviews: *Booklist, Kirkus Reviews, Publishers Weekly*
- Rainbow Book List, 2023

Conversation Starters
1. When you're at a parade, would you rather watch or be a part of the parade?
2. What's your favorite part of a parade?
3. Can you draw a float or a balloon that you might see in a parade?

'Twas the Night before Pride by Joanna McClintick, illustrated by Juana Medina. Candlewick Press, 2022. (Q)

While there are many books about Pride parades and celebrations, this one also discusses the history of Pride, including what LGBTQIA+ communities have gone through to get to this point, such as the Stonewall Riots and the AIDS crisis.

Conversation Starters
1. What does *pride* mean to you?
2. What can you do at Pride?

What Are Your Words? A Book about Pronouns by Katherine Locke, illustrated by Anne/Andy Passchier. Little, Brown Books for Young Readers, 2021. (T, Q)

Sometimes people's pronouns change, and every time Ari's Uncle Lior visits, they ask what Ari's words are. Ari finds out that sometimes it takes some work to figure out your pronouns, and that it's okay if they evolve or shift.

Awards and Honors
• Starred review: *School Library Journal*

Conversation Starters
1. What are your pronouns?
2. What other words can you use to describe yourself?

When Aidan Became a Brother by Kyle Lukoff, illustrated by Kaylani Juanita. Lee and Low Books, 2019. (T)

Aidan's parents think he's a girl, but he knows that inside he's a boy. It was hard to tell his parents, but when they tell him they're expecting another baby, Aidan makes sure that his parents will be inclusive for his new sibling and not assume the new baby's gender.

Awards and Honors
- Starred reviews: *Booklist, Kirkus Reviews, Publishers Weekly, School Library Journal*
- NCTE Charlotte Huck Award for Outstanding Fiction for Children Honor Book, 2020
- Stonewall Book Award–Mike Morgan and Larry Romans Children's Literature Award, 2020

Conversation Starters
1. Are you an older sibling? What is it like having a younger sibling?
2. Did it make a difference to you whether your sibling was a boy or a girl?

PICTURE BOOK NONFICTION

ABC Pride by Louie Stowell and Elly Barnes, illustrated by Amy Phelps. DK Children, 2022. (Q)

Children of any age can learn from and enjoy this alphabet book that includes entries for flags, love, and nonbinary people, among others. The flag page specifically offers more than just the standard few pride flags, including the aromantic pride flag and the intersex pride flag, and the entry for love is inclusive of aromantic people, noting that "not everyone falls in love."

Awards and Honors
- Rainbow Book List, 2023

Conversation Starters
1. Is there anybody who looks like you in the pictures?
2. What is one thing you learned from this book?

Being You: A First Conversation about Gender by Megan Madison and Jessica Ralli, illustrated by Anne/Andy Passchier. Rise X Penguin Workshop, 2021. (Q)

This board book provides a very basic start for caregivers in discussing issues of gender, bodies, and pronouns with the children in their care.

Awards and Honors
- Starred review: *Kirkus Reviews*

Conversation Starters
1. What colors do you like to wear?
2. What words make you happy?

The Big Book of Pride Flags by Jessica Kingsley Publishers, illustrated by Jem Milton. Jessica Kingsley Publishers, 2022. (Q)

Told in simple language, this book shares many of the current and several historical pride flags, along with brief explanations of what each one symbolizes.

Awards and Honors
- Rainbow Book List, 2023

Conversation Starters
1. Where do you see flags in your neighborhood?
2. What kind of flags do you see?

Drawing On Walls: A Story of Keith Haring by Matthew Burgess, illustrated by Josh Cochran. Enchanted Lion Books, 2020. (G)

This beautifully illustrated book tells the story of artist Keith Haring from his childhood to his early death from AIDS and all his wonderful, brilliant life in between. He and his dad would draw together by creating line drawings, taking turns drawing lines and adding to each other's creations to change one thing to another. He loved working with children because they understood what he was doing and he loved their creativity. This book talks about his relationship with his partner Juan DuBose and how happy they were together. Included are author's notes, biographical notes, and direct quotes from Keith Haring.

Awards and Honors
- Starred reviews: *Booklist, Publishers Weekly, School Library Journal*
- NCTE Orbis Pictus Award for Outstanding Nonfiction for Children nominee, 2021

Conversation Starters
1. Why do you think Keith loves drawing on walls?
2. What is your favorite part of this book and why?

If You're a Kid Like Gavin by Gavin Grimm and Kyle Lukoff, illustrated by J Yang. Katherine Tegen Books, 2022. (T)

This picture book biography of Gavin Grimm talks about his experiences growing up, coming out, and advocating for himself and other trans kids trying to get adequate bathroom access.

Awards and Honors
- Starred reviews: *Kirkus Reviews, Publishers Weekly*
- Rainbow Book List, 2023

Conversation Starters
1. Why should you advocate for yourself or others if you see an inequity?
2. Have you ever had someone keep you from entering the bathroom? If so, how did you handle it?

Pink, Blue, and You: Questions for Kids about Gender Stereotypes by Elise Gravel with Mykaell Blais. Anne Schwartz Books, 2022. (Q)

While mostly about, and breaking, gender stereotypes, this book also delves into various gender identities, body differences, and pronouns and even talks briefly about some people being labeled as intersex.

Awards and Honors
- Starred review: *School Library Journal*

Conversation Starters
1. Are all of your friends the same?
2. What gender stereotypes do you break?

The Pronoun Book by Chris Ayala-Kronos, illustrated by Melita Tirado. Clarion Books, 2022. (T)

A board book is not necessarily the best format for an introduction to pronouns, but this simple text and repeated messaging about asking what someone's pronouns are provides a very early entry point to pronouns and gender that can be built upon as readers grow.

Awards and Honors
• Rainbow Book List, 2023

Conversation Starters
1. What are your pronouns?
2. Can you introduce yourself with your name and pronouns?
3. How can you ask somebody what their pronouns are?

Sewing the Rainbow by Gayle E. Pitman, illustrated by Holly Clifton-Brown. Magination Press, 2018. (G)

Gilbert Baker grew up in Kansas but moved to San Francisco after the draft when he refused to carry a weapon. In San Francisco, he felt like he could finally breathe. In 1978, Harvey Milk and Gilbert Baker decided that the gay community needed a better symbol than the pink triangle, and Gilbert designed the original rainbow pride flag.

Conversation Starters
1. What is your favorite color?
2. What other symbols do you know?

Sharice's Big Voice: A Native Kid Becomes a Congresswoman by Sharice Davids and Nancy K. Mays, illustrated by Joshua Mangeshig Pawis-Steckley. HarperCollins, 2021. (L)

When Sharice was young, she never thought she would run for Congress, let alone win. In doing so, she became one of the first Native American women in Congress. In this powerful story of perseverance and triumph, Sharice shares her journey of how she accomplished her goal of being one of the first Native American congresswomen and the first lesbian representative from Kansas by forging her own path and by overcoming the obstacles and doubters (including herself) along the way.

Awards and Honors
- Starred review: *Kirkus Reviews*
- ALSC Notable Children's Book for Middle Readers, 2022

Conversation Starters
1. What two things does Sharice do to make friends?
2. What is something you accomplished even when someone (including yourself) did not believe you could do it?

Strong by Rob Kearney and Eric Rosswood, illustrated by Nidhi Chanani. Little, Brown Books for Young Readers, 2022. (G)

Rob Kearney is the only out gay strongman. After learning the sport and competing while fitting in with everyone else, wearing boring, monochrome clothing, but not doing well, he finds someone to encourage him and the confidence to wear brighter clothes in competition, which helps him win.

Awards and Honors
- Stonewall Book Awards–Mike Morgan and Larry Romans Children's Literature Honor, 2023
- Rainbow Book List, 2023

Conversation Starters
1. What are the ways Rob is strong?
2. What is something you do to inspire your own confidence?

Two Grooms on a Cake: The Story of America's First Gay Wedding
by Rob Sanders, illustrated by Robbie Cathro. Little Bee Books, 2021.
(G)

This very accessible story that explains a gay couple's quest to marry is told by the grooms on the wedding cake, who explain the issues and steps for the marriage equality time line. Illustrated in soft colors that give the reader a visual understanding of what went into the New York Marriage Equality Act, this is a great read-aloud that contains author's notes and pictures of the real-life couple, as well as a time line.

Awards and Honors
- Starred review: *Kirkus Reviews*

Conversation Starters
1. Have you ever been to a wedding? Or been a part of one?
2. Do you know everything that has to get done for a wedding?

ACTIVITIES, PROJECTS, AND PROGRAMS FOR YOUNG READERS

Pride Flags
Using the books *Pride Colors, The Big Book of Pride Flags, Sewing the Rainbow,* and others as the basis for this project, share a variety of books about pride flags and the ways they bring a community together. Have children discuss any flags they have seen. What colors are in the flags? What do the colors in the flags mean? Ask children to draw a picture of the flag they would like to share, using colors that mean something to them. Display the finished products in the library!

Shadow Work
After reading the book *My Shadow Is Purple,* allow children to draw a picture of themselves and choose the color they want their shadow to be. Have children get in smaller circles to talk about the colors they chose and why. Have each child then add a sentence to their picture that explains the color they chose.

Create a basket with other books about choosing colors to mean something. Some choices might include *My Rainbow; The Day the Crayons Quit* (Philomel Books, 2013); *Pink, Blue, and You: Questions for Kids about Gender Stereotypes; Red: A Crayon's Story* (Greenwillow Books, 2015); and *Pink Is for Boys* (Running Press Kids, 2018). Make sure this basket is accessible during any free reading time.

Welcome Book
After reading *Sharice's Big Voice: A Native Kid Becomes a Congresswoman,* begin a discussion about friendship. Ask students if they have ever been the new kid. Make a list of ways they felt. After reading additional books, *All Are Welcome* (Knopf Books for Young Readers, 2018), *Calvin,* or *Neither* (Little, Brown Books for Young Readers, 2018), and using the list of ways the group felt as their template, work with children to create a Welcome Book demonstrating all the ways they will make someone new feel welcome in their class.

WRAP-UP

Many excellent books deal with LGBTQIA+ issues on a very early level. Any or all would be useful in sharing with young children as you have conversations about similarities and differences, families and friends. We are all different in some ways and yet the same in others, and the uniqueness of each is to be celebrated.

The common thread in all of these books is that acceptance and caring are what matters. As we teach our children about fairness and equality, it is important to be sure we are unbiased in our presentations. Children are curious, and they will want to know why one friend's family differs from theirs. They may not be immune to the prejudice displayed around them but can still understand the rational explanation that differences are acceptable. Friends are to be gauged by the way they treat one another, not by the way they look or dress.

Books like these should be available to classrooms, on library bookshelves, and in your read-aloud stack. They will only deepen the understanding and empathy of your students for one another.

NOTES

1. Rudine Sims Bishop, "Mirrors, Windows, and Sliding Glass Doors," *Perspectives* 6, no. 3 (1990), ix–xi.
2. Nina Garcia, "Children's Books about Family," Sleeping Should Be Easy (website), December 1, 2022, https://sleepingshouldbeeasy.com/childrens-books-about-family/.
3. Mary Ellen Flannery, "Why We Need Diverse Books," NEA, October 26, 2020, under "Empathy Is Key," www.nea.org/advocating-for-change/new-from-nea/why-we-need-diverse-books.
4. "Heather Has Two Mommies," LesleaKids.com, under "Why I Wrote This Book," https://lesleakids.com/books-for-kids-teens/picture-books/heather-has-two-mommies/.
5. "Rainbow Round Table (RRT)," American Library Association, www.ala.org/rt/rrt.

Books and Conversation for Middle Grade Readers

Younger children are focused on learning about the world around them and how they fit into it. Middle grade children and tweens go a step further to discover who they are, how they fit in with friends, and how they want to express themselves. Ellen in *Ellen Outside the Lines* already knows that she's autistic, but it takes going to Spain to discover that she's more interested in girls than boys and to start questioning gender. Hazel in *Hazel's Theory of Evolution* is used to having two moms, but as she sees friends and classmates develop crushes, she feels left out, until one of her moms tells her that it's okay not to have crushes or fall in love or get married or have kids.

||||||||||||||||||||||||||

Start Small
The First Middle Grade Books to Add to Your Collection

- *Into the Tall, Tall Grass* by Loriel Ryon
- *The Civil War of Amos Abernathy* by Michael Leali
- *The Best Liars in Riverview* by Lin Thompson

||||||||||||||||||||||

Authors Speak Out
Brandon T. Snider

When I was a kid there was no LGBTQIA+ representation that I could see. If anything, queer people were the butt of a joke, and slurs were used in TV and film like it was nothing. Now visibility is at an all-time high, which is amazing, but the work is not done. We still have a long way to go. What I try to do with my work is let LGBTQIA+ kids know they're not alone. They deserve to be included and feel included. . . . It's important that LGBTQIA+ stories be more than just one thing, so I always try to strike a balance. . . . Educators need to go to bat for LGBTQIA+ youth in force and make sure they're not keeping a seat saved for homophobia as if it were just another opinion that deserves space. There are still many gaps to bridge. That's why it's also important for libraries to carry LGBTQIA+ books and encourage everyone to read them. Sharing our stories is how we understand one another and move forward.

TRENDS IN LGBTQIA+ MIDDLE GRADE

Publishing is starting to see a lot more books featuring queer kids and kids exploring gender, and a lot fewer books whose only queer content is showing queer adults or side characters. Older elementary school and middle school children are beginning to branch out with more authentic and intersectional identities, both in the books they choose to read and in how they present themselves.

||||||||||||||||||||||

Voices from the Stacks
Meaghan Hummel

So much of my childhood revolved around stories—a favorite book that my grandmother would read to me, post-birthday trips to the bookstore with gifted money, staying up late reading when I was supposed to be sleeping. Books have power in our lives. They teach us, entertain us, help us to grow. Today, more than ever, books and media have the power to help society grow in acceptance and care for one another. As an educator of ancient history, my overarching goal is to help my students grow as humans by providing them with an opportunity to learn more about the world around them, and how we made it to this point, so they can be a greater part of it in the future. As a queer educator, I know that teaching my students to take up their place in the world means they have to feel seen first. Being able to provide my students with books that represent them empowers me to help them in self-discovery. Watching them relate to characters who are like them brings me great joy and hope for the future. LGBTQIA+ books are, without exaggeration, a life-changing and sometimes lifesaving tool for our queer kids, and I am so glad to have resources to seek out so I can put them on my shelf.

SPECIAL FOCUS: IDENTITY

In 2012 it was notable that a middle grade graphic novel, *Drama* by Raina Telgemeier, featured a friend-level character who was gay and was named a Stonewall Honor Book.

Now, a decade later, we have many middle grade books featuring main characters who are not just gay or lesbian but transgender, nonbinary, and even intersex. These books provide not only a window from which kids can see others different from themselves but also that sliding door which allows them to discover if this is who they might be.

MIDDLE GRADE BOOKS THAT CAN BE USED IN OTHER DISPLAYS

Black History Month	
In the Key of Us	*King and the Dragonflies*

Hispanic Heritage Month	
Into the Tall, Tall Grass	*The One Who Loves You the Most*

Asian American and Pacific Islander Month	
The Best at It	*Obie Is Man Enough*
Nikhil Out Loud	

(continued on next page)

MIDDLE GRADE BOOKS THAT CAN BE USED IN OTHER DISPLAYS
(cont'd)

Veterans Day
The Civil War of Amos Abernathy

Summer

Almost Flying	*The Language of Seabirds*
The Best Liars in Riverview	*The Mighty Heart of Sunny St. James*
Drum Roll, Please	*Too Bright to See*
Frankie and Bug	

Autism Acceptance Month
Ellen Outside the Lines

GRAPHIC NOVELS

Beetle and the Hollowbones by Aliza Layne. Atheneum Books for Young Readers, 2020. (L)

Beetle, a goblin-witch, has lost contact with her best friend Kat Hollowbone. Kat left to go to a special school for magic training, and when Beetle realizes that Kat is back along with her domineering aunt, Beetle wonders if they can pick up where they left off. Beetle's friend, since Kat has been away, is Blob Ghost. Blob Ghost is unable to leave the town's mall, but when Kat's aunt reveals that she is tearing it down, they must find a way to save Blob Ghost before they get destroyed along with the mall. By the end, Beetle and Kat realize their feelings are not only friendship, and they share a sweet kiss.

Awards and Honors
- Starred reviews: *Booklist, Kirkus Reviews, Publishers Weekly, School Library Journal*
- Stonewall Honor Book in Children's Literature, 2021

Conversation Starters
1. How do you feel about the way Kat's aunt treats her?
2. If you could have one magical power, what would it be and why?
3. Have you ever lost contact with a friend and then reconnected? How did it go?

Other Boys by Damian Alexander. First Second, 2021. (G)

Damian's plan to avoid bullying is to stay completely silent, but in middle school, any differences, real or perceived, are immediate targets. The boys at Damian's school are mean, and he can't figure out why he has a crush on one of them.

Awards and Honors
- Starred review: *Booklist*
- Rainbow Book List, 2023

Conversation Starters
1. Have you ever had a crush on somebody even if they weren't very nice?
2. What have you done to avoid getting bullied?

The Prince and the Dressmaker by Jen Wang. First Second, 2018. (Q)

Prince Sebastian's family would like for him to find a bride, but he's too busy protecting his secret—at night he goes out in fabulous clothes and is known as the fashion trendsetter Lady Crystallia! His best friend Frances and her wonderful seamstress skills continually raise the bar for Parisian couture attire, but the cost of keeping his secret wears on her. When Sebastian's family finds out the truth, everyone must come to their own realizations about forgiveness, love, and acceptance.

Awards and Honors
- Starred reviews: *Booklist, Horn Book, Publishers Weekly, School Library Journal*
- Eisner Award, 2018
- Harvey Award for Best Children's or Young Adult Book, 2018
- Harvey Award Book of the Year nominee, 2018

- Goodreads Choice Award, Graphic Novels and Comics nominee, 2018
- Prix du Festival d'Angoulême for Prix jeunesse, 2019
- Rhode Island Teen Book Award nominee, 2020
- Rebecca Caudill Young Readers' Book Award nominee, 2020

Conversation Starters

1. Why does Frances decide she can't make dresses for Sebastian anymore? What has happened before to make her feel that way?
2. Compare Sebastian's character when he is drawn as Lady Crystallia and when he is dressed as the prince. What changes can you see, both in the art and in his personality? What reason do you think the author has for highlighting those changes?

MAGICAL REALISM

Cattywampus by Ash Van Otterloo. Scholastic, 2020. (I)

Delpha and Katybird both want to learn magic, and Delpha has found her family's secret book of hexes. The only problem is that Delpha's and Katybird's families have been feuding for ages. When they accidentally release a hex that turns all of their dead relatives into zombies, they'll have to put aside their differences and work together.

Conversation Starters

1. Are there any other big family feuds that you know about?
2. What would you do with a book of hexes?

Into the Tall, Tall Grass by Loriel Ryon. Margaret K. McElderry Books, 2020. (L)

Yolanda is an ordinary teenager with a not-so-ordinary family. The Rodriguez women have unique gifts, with the exception of Yolanda. Even her twin sister, Sonja, has a magical gift, so Yolanda instead focuses on her passion for science. Her Welo (grandpa) spent his life studying science, trying to understand the gifts of the Rodriguez family. When Welo passes away, Yolanda is left saddened that she could not find a cure for him. Then, her

Wela (grandma) becomes sick, and Yolanda is desperate to save her. Yolanda, Sonja, Wela, and their friends embark on a journey to save Wela before it is too late. However, along the way, Yolanda and her sister begin to learn the story of their Wela and the Rodriguez family. They soon discover that the journey they set out on is not the one they anticipated, and they will also discover the true meaning of their magic.

Awards and Honors
- Starred review: *School Library Journal*

Conversation Starters
1. Why do you think Yolanda received her gift later than her twin sister, Sonja?
2. What were Wela's true intentions behind having her granddaughters bring her to the pecan tree? Do you think Wela knew what would happen to the pecan orchard when they completed their journey?
3. Why do you think Yolanda had a difficult time at first accepting the relationship between Sonja and her former best friend, Ghita?
4. Why do you think that Ghita and Hasik accepted Yolanda and Sonja's family and their gifts so easily when others in their town could not?
5. If you could have a magical gift like Yolanda and Sonja, what would you choose and why?

Moonflower by Kacen Callender. Scholastic Press, 2022. (T, Nonbinary)

While struggling with depression, Moon travels between the physical world and the spirit realm each night, hoping each time to find a way to stay.

Awards and Honors
- Starred review: *Publishers Weekly*
- Rainbow Book List Top Ten for Young Readers, 2023

Conversation Starters
1. What do you do when you feel like something is too difficult to talk about?
2. Where do you go when you want to be alone?

|||||||||||||||||||||||

Authors You Should Know
Kacen Callender

Callender's work is admirable for a variety of reasons, particularly how deeply they have examined the experience of being an LGBTQ+ young person from a variety of backgrounds and maturity levels, both age-related maturity and the sort that comes from trauma. Callender's young people are always fully realized characters who resonate with readers and accurately portray the way those young people (and young people in general) grow and change internally as they go through various situations. The trajectories of self-recognition and self-acceptance followed by Callender's main characters are ultimately hopeful and buoyant, yet the books' endings are realistic and never oversimplified, acknowledging the complexities and difficulties of being an LGBTQ+ young person in a confusing and often hostile environment.

Callender's works are a valuable addition to libraries and classrooms for all children. Deep character development, a gentle touch in handling trauma and emotions, and a smoothly plotted narrative that is entertaining and illuminative are hallmarks of Callender's work, and their books are also excellent examples of literary prowess outside of their representation. The LGBTQ+ representation contained in each of Callender's works is normalizing and considered; it strikes a great balance between allowing non-queer students a window into the difficulties faced by queer young people and being a mirror for those queer young people who have had to face judgment and bigotry in all its forms. These sorts of books can contribute greatly toward normalizing the existence of LGBTQ+ people in a community or classroom, and they can help all students feel secure in their inclusion. Callender's books cover a wide range of reading levels, ages, and maturity levels, making them appropriate for a large number of readers.

—ALLIE STEVENS

The Vanquishers by Kalynn Bayron. Bloomsbury Children's Books, 2022. (T, G)

All of the vampires were wiped out years ago by the elite vampire hunting team known as the Vanquishers. Most people have stopped taking precautions by now, but Boog's parents and their friends are still careful with vampire-proofing, avoiding being out after dark, and taking other precautions. When one of Boog's friends goes missing at a school event and the new school counselor is acting weird, Boog and the rest of the squad are on the case.

Awards and Honors
- Starred review: *Publishers Weekly*

Conversation Starters
1. What would you do if you knew vampires were real?
2. What precautions would you take to be safe?

NONFICTION

Pride: An Inspirational History of the LGBTQ+ Movement by Stella Caldwell. Penguin Workshop, 2022. (Q)

Although originally published in the United Kingdom in 2020, the American edition does have country-specific resources in the back matter. It is designed for younger readers, so while it does give an overview of the quest for rights, it leaves out a considerable amount, though unlike US publications it includes information from around the globe.

Awards and Honors
- Starred reviews: *Kirkus Reviews, School Library Journal*
- Rainbow Book List, 2023

Conversation Starters
1. What are some differences between the history and rights of the LGBTQIA+ communities in the United Kingdom and in the United States?
2. Was anything noted in this book surprising to you?

Rainbow Revolutionaries: Fifty LGBTQ+ People Who Made History by **Sarah Prager, illustrated by Sarah Papworth. Harper, 2022. (Q)**

The author notes that this is a follow-up to, and middle grade version of, Prager's 2017 *Queer, There, and Everywhere: 23 People Who Changed the World*. The biographies are brief and abridged but suited to the age level, and the author includes back matter such as a glossary, time line, and guide to flags and identity symbols.

Conversation Starters
1. Who was the most interesting to read about and why?
2. What do you like about this book's format?

What Is the AIDS Crisis? by **Nico Medina, illustrated by Tim Foley. Penguin Workshop, 2022. (Q)**

In light of the COVID-19 pandemic, Nico Medina wrote *What Is the AIDS Crisis?* for younger readers. It traces the time line of the crisis from the first cases with Kaposi's sarcoma to present-day preventative medications, treatment options, and the few cases of people who have been cured, though it focuses primarily on the impact on gay men. The book includes time lines and a bibliography.

Conversation Starters
1. What comparisons can you make between AIDS and other pandemics or health crises?
2. What is one thing you learned from this book?

REALISTIC FICTION

Almost Flying by **Jake Maia Arlow. Dial Books for Young Readers, 2021. (L, G, B)**

Dalia has just found out that her dad is dating someone new. He's been a little less involved in her life for the past year, since her mother moved away and they moved into a little apartment in Long Island. He hasn't even noticed that she's not friends with Abby anymore, much less that she's made a new friend at swim practice. But first Dalia finds out about the girlfriend, then that they've been dating for six months, then that the girlfriend has a daughter in college named Alexa, and then that the two of them are engaged! It's an outrage. As a bonding activity, the parents decide that Alexa should take Dalia on her summer road trip to amusement parks, and since Alexa's bringing a friend, Dalia convinces the parents she should be able to invite the new girl from swim practice, Rani, as well. While riding roller coasters together, it's not just the height and the thrills making her stomach feel fluttery.

Awards and Honors
- Stonewall Honor Book in Children's Literature, 2022

Conversation Starters
1. How is a crush like riding a roller coaster?
2. Have you had to adjust to a blended family? Or has one of your friends?

|||||||||||||||||||||||||

Voices from the Stacks
Katy Hume

Almost Flying, by Jake Maia Arlow, is the book I needed when I was thirteen and totally not crushing on Angelina Jolie in *Tomb Raider*. The protagonist, Dalia, is in a similar situation of totally not crushing on her new friend, Rani. It takes a road trip with her soon-to-be-stepsister Alexa and Alexa's girlfriend for Dalia to confront the scary new things she's feeling about Rani and accept them for what they are.

Dalia's inner monologue kept me chuckling throughout the book because she used all the same excuses for her feelings that I did when I was a middle schooler barricading the closet door from the inside. But unlike teenage me, Dalia feels safe enough to (eventually) accept those excuses as the denial they are, with some help from Alexa and her new friends. Twenty years ago, *gay* was an insult kids hurled at each other in the hallways or a scandalous rumor you heard about an upperclassman who mysteriously stopped coming to school. *Gay* and everything that came with it was why thirteen-year-old Katy tore up her *Tomb Raider* poster and buried who she was for years.

Reading *Almost Flying* as an adult felt like going back in time and breaking down the closet door. The heart of the story is the affirmation I never got as a teenager: that being gay doesn't make you weird or a freak or any less worthy of being happy. Better yet, the thirteen-year-olds of today struggling with the same feelings I had so long ago now have books like *Almost Flying* to guide their way and reassure them that they're not alone.

Ana on the Edge by A. J. Sass. Little, Brown Books for Young Readers, 2020. (T, Nonbinary)

Ana loves figure skating and is one of the best, but how can she tell her mother that she hates the princess-themed program after they've made so many sacrifices for Ana's skating, much less explain why she's so uncomfortable with it?

Awards and Honors
- Starred review: *Booklist*
- Rainbow Book List Top Ten for Young Readers, 2021

Conversation Starters
1. How does Ana experience social dysphoria?
2. Does Ana's ability to perform while skating parallel efforts to perform gender?

Answers in the Pages by David Levithan. Random House Kids Publishing, 2022. (G)

Donavon likes school and his fifth-grade teacher, Mr. Howe, who gives the class a new book to read for language arts. When Don takes it home and leaves it on the kitchen counter to make a snack, his mother picks it up and reads the last page. Thus begins the snowball effect of a book challenge, and this book walks through the correct way to handle them. Through Levithan's deft storytelling, we not only learn about Donavon, his classmates, and their feelings about the book and gay characters, but we also get peeks inside the story that started this event.

Awards and Honors
- Starred reviews: *Publishers Weekly, School Library Journal*
- Rainbow Book List, 2023

Conversation Starters
1. What causes a book to get challenged?
2. Should students have a voice?

The Best at It by Maulik Pancholy. Balzer+Bray, 2019. (G)

Rahul feels very different from most of his classmates. He's Indian American in a small town, struggles with anxiety, is bullied, and faces racial prejudice. When his grandfather encourages him to find something that he is "the best at," he tries to figure out what that might be, and if he can get his crush, Justin, to notice him.

Awards and Honors
- Starred reviews: *Booklist, Kirkus Reviews, Publishers Weekly*
- Stonewall Honor Book in Children's Literature, 2020
- Rebecca Caudill Young Readers' Book Award, 2023

Conversation Starters
1. What are you the best at?
2. Does your best friend stand by you the way that Rahul's best friend Chelsea does?

The Best Liars in Riverview by Lin Thompson. Little, Brown, 2022. (Q, G)

After a disastrous school year filled with bullying from both classmates and a parent, Joel and Aubrey part ways during the middle of a campout. While Aubrey goes home, Joel is nowhere to be found the next morning, sparking a frantic search. Aubrey knows something but isn't sure how many of Joel's secrets are safe to tell.

Awards and Honors
- Starred review: *Booklist*
- Rainbow Book List, 2023

Conversation Starters
1. What kinds of games do you play with your friends?
2. Is there a way Aubrey could have helped Joel before he went missing?

Candidly Cline by Kathryn Ormsbee. HarperCollins Children's Books, 2021. (L, B)

Cline Alden comes from a very musically oriented family; her mother named her after country singer Patsy Cline. But her mama has lost the music now that she has to take on so many extra shifts at the diner to take care of Cline and Cline's grandma, who's been diagnosed with Alzheimer's. When another waitress at the diner hands Cline a flyer for a singer-songwriter workshop at the University of Kentucky, she knows she'll do whatever it takes to go. She can't come up with the $300 tuition fee, so she tries haggling at the check-in desk, like her mom does when bills pile up, and ends up in tears before she's finally let in; but a girl her age saw her cry, and she's mortified. So when the workshop instructor assigns everyone partners, naturally Cline is partnered with the girl who saw her cry, Sylvie. But maybe the teacher is on to something, because by the next session, they start to click in more ways than one.

Awards and Honors
- Starred reviews: *Kirkus Reviews, Publishers Weekly, School Library Journal*
- Rainbow Book List, 2023

Conversation Starters
1. Cline's all about country music, and Sylvie loves rock. What five songs or artists would you put on a list to help someone get to know you?
2. Would you be confident enough to talk your way into something you really wanted?

The Civil War of Amos Abernathy by Michael Leali. Harper, 2022. (G)

Eighth grader Amos Abernathy has been volunteering at the Living History Park for as far back as he can remember; his mom runs it. When another kid his age, Ben, starts volunteering at the park and can answer all of Amos's questions about Abraham Lincoln, he knows Ben is special. But after talking one day with his best friend Chloe and his new friend Ben, they realize that all of the history they reenact at LHP is from the perspective of white, straight, cisgender people, usually men. And when the opportunity to propose a new exhibit at the park arises, the kids gather all of their resources and research to prepare an exhibit on the forgotten voices of history.

Awards and Honors
- Starred reviews: *Booklist, School Library Journal*
- Rainbow Book List Top Ten for Young Readers, 2023

Conversation Starters
1. How much do you know about historical *queeroes*?
2. Using your library or research skills, can you find more information about any of the people that Amos and his friends talk about at the end of the book?

Different Kinds of Fruit by Kyle Lukoff. Dial Books for Young Readers, 2022. (Q, Nonbinary, T)

Right before the first day of sixth grade, Annabelle's dad is rattled when Annabelle finds a flyer for a Pre-Pride Drag Brunch in Seattle. Annabelle puts it out of her head until she comes home from school talking about a new student in her class, Bailey, who is nonbinary and uses they/them pronouns. Both of Annabelle's parents freak out, and she doesn't know why. Are they homophobic or transphobic? As Annabelle and Bailey become close friends, everything eventually comes out.

Awards and Honors
- Starred reviews: *Booklist, School Library Journal*
- Rainbow Book List Top Ten for Young Readers, 2023

Conversation Starters
1. Were you surprised to find out about Annabelle's parents?
2. How do attitudes about LGBTQIA+ identities change between generations?

Drum Roll, Please by Lisa Jenn Bigelow. HarperCollins, 2018. (B)

Melly and her best friend, Olivia, are off to music camp for the summer, and Melly is hoping it will be enough of a distraction from her parents' impending divorce. When the girls aren't put in the same band, Melly starts to worry— Olivia was the only reason Melly started playing the drums in the first place. But when they start making friends with other campers, and developing crushes on bandmates, Melly doesn't know how Olivia will react to her budding relationship with Adeline.

Awards and Honors
• Starred reviews: *Publishers Weekly, School Library Journal*
• Rebecca Caudill Young Readers' Book Award, 2021

Conversation Starters
1. Is it scary when you're separated from your best friend at a camp?
2. If you were a type of music, what would you be?

Ellen Outside the Lines by A. J. Sass. Little, Brown Books for Young Readers, 2022. (Q, Nonbinary)

Ellen Katz is excited to go on a class trip to Barcelona with her best and only friend, Laurel, but they've been drifting apart recently, and despite being roommates on the trip, they're assigned to different groups for the scavenger hunt. Instead, Ellen's on a team with two boys and a new kid, Isa, who's nonbinary. As they all discover landmarks in the city, they also learn new things about themselves and one another.

Awards and Honors
• Starred review: *Booklist*
• Sydney Taylor Book Award, Middle Grade Honor, 2023
• Rainbow Book List Top Ten for Young Readers, 2023

Conversation Starters

1. Ellen notices patterns in their life, like the *el* in both *Ellen* and *Laurel*. What patterns have you found in your life?
2. Have you been forced to meet and work with others unknown to you? How did it work out?

Frankie and Bug by Gayle Forman. Aladdin, 2021. (T, G)

Bug just wants to go to the beach all summer while her mom works, but her older brother doesn't want her tagging along, so she's stuck entertaining her neighbor's nephew. Soon they're investigating the case of the Midnight Marauder, which leads the two to discoveries about themselves and each other.

Awards and Honors

- Starred reviews: *Booklist, School Library Journal*

Conversation Starters

1. What do you like to do during the summer?
2. Have you ever been stuck entertaining a younger person? How did it turn out?

Hazel Hill Is Gonna Win This One by Maggie Horne. Clarion, 2022. (L)

Hazel is sure that Ella Quinn is her nemesis after she beat Hazel in the speech competition last year. When they start talking after Tyler tells Hazel that Ella Quinn told him she has a crush on her, Hazel finally listens to what Ella Quinn has to say, and she's not so sure who really deserves to be her nemesis. With this year's speech competition, maybe the biggest unsolved mystery (Hazel's chosen topic) isn't the Black Dahlia or Jack the Ripper, but why everyone believes Tyler over Hazel and Ella.

Awards and Honors

- Starred review: *Kirkus Reviews*

Conversation Starters

1. What would you write a speech about?
2. Have you ever had a nemesis? A competition that you imagine?

Hazel's Theory of Evolution by Lisa Jenn Bigelow. HarperCollins, 2019. (A, L, T)

Hazel would rather get lost in the pages of an encyclopedia than deal with the mounting changes in her life: starting over at a new school in her last year of middle school, worrying about her mom's pregnancy following two miscarriages, and questioning romantic attraction as other girls focus on boys.

Awards and Honors
- Starred review: *Booklist*
- Lambda Literary Award for Children and Young Adults, 2020

Conversation Starters
1. What are your favorite farm animals?
2. What have you felt pressured about because "everyone else is doing it"?

In the Key of Us by Mariama J. Lockington. Farrar, Straus and Giroux Books for Young Readers, 2022. (Q, L)

Harmony Music Camp is a place where Andi, Zora, and other kids can be themselves and lose themselves in music. Andi and Zora are bunkmates in their cabin, and everyone assumes they'll be close friends just because they're both Black. But they have vastly different reasons for being at camp. Andi lost her mom the first day of school and has been living with her aunt and uncle, who are now expecting a baby of their own. Music was a way for Andi to connect with her mother, and she's feeling like she's lost the melody. Zora's parents are always pushing her to be the very best first-chair flute every week, but she doesn't love it like she used to, and she misses dancing. Over the four weeks of summer, in a story told from alternating points of view, the girls learn more about themselves and each other.

Awards and Honors
- Starred reviews: *Kirkus Reviews, Publishers Weekly, School Library Journal*
- Stonewall Book Awards–Mike Morgan and Larry Romans Children's Literature Honor, 2023
- Rainbow Book List, 2023

Conversation Starters
1. What kinds of music speak to your soul?
2. How do you use art to express yourself?

Ivy Aberdeen's Letter to the World by Ashley Herring Blake. Little, Brown Books for Young Readers, 2018 (L)

Ivy's house is completely destroyed in a tornado, and she feels like she's lost everything. But when her notebook filled with drawings of girls holding hands disappears, and the pictures show up in her locker one by one, she doesn't know what to think, except that she might have a crush on a girl in her class.

Awards and Honors
- Starred reviews: *Kirkus Reviews, Publishers Weekly, School Library Journal*
- Stonewall Honor Book, 2019

Conversation Starters
1. If you had to seek shelter from a tornado and had time to grab only one thing, what would it be?
2. Have you ever had a secret you felt like you couldn't tell anyone?

Jude Saves the World by Ronnie Riley. Scholastic, 2023. (Nonbinary, B, G)

When Stevie gets kicked out of the popular girls' group by Tessa and rumors swirl that the reason why is that Stevie has a crush on another girl, Jude and Dallas open up their queer circle to Stevie. Jude is struggling with being more open about their gender and bisexuality, and Dallas is dealing with his parents fighting constantly and how to come out to them and his sisters as gay. Providing a safe space for Stevie leads Jude to start a Safe Space group at the local library, not just for queer youth, but for anybody who feels marginalized.

Conversation Starters

1. Is it Jude's responsibility not only to provide a safe space but to save the world?
2. How would you support a classmate who gets dropped by their friend group?

King and the Dragonflies by Kacen Callender. Scholastic, 2020. (Q, G)

Kingston's older brother Khalid has died, and Kingston's sure he's now a dragonfly. King wants to talk to his best friend, but Sandy's missing, and shortly before he died, Khalid told him to stop being friends with Sandy. When King finds Sandy living in a tent to escape his abusive father, the boys have to find ways to live with their situations and support each other.

Awards and Honors

- Starred reviews: *Booklist, Horn Book, Publishers Weekly, School Library Journal*
- Goodreads Choice Award, Best Middle Grade and Children's nominee, 2020
- National Book Award for Young People's Literature, 2020
- Coretta Scott King Book Award, Author nominee, 2021
- Walter Dean Myers Award, Younger Readers Category nominee, 2021
- Lambda Literary Award for LGBTQ Children's/Middle Grade, 2021
- Rebecca Caudill Young Readers' Book Award, 2022

Conversation Starters

1. What would you do if you found out your best friend had run away from home?
2. If you knew a friend was being abused, what would you do?

The Language of Seabirds by Will Taylor. Scholastic Press, 2022. (G)

When Jeremy's parents divorce, he and his dad travel to the Oregon coast to stay at an uncle's cabin for two weeks while his mom moves out. His dad's expectations of him keep changing, and he knows he has to keep his love of fashion magazines to himself. The first day, he discovers both a book on identifying local birds and a boy about his

own age running along the beach. Soon both the book and the boy become more important to him than he would have ever thought.

Awards and Honors
- Starred reviews: *Kirkus Reviews, Publishers Weekly*
- Rainbow Book List, 2023

Conversation Starters
1. What birds are in your area?
2. Have you ever decided to try something just because you wanted to spend time with someone?
3. What words would the names of birds mean to you in your own language?

The Mighty Heart of Sunny St. James by Ashley Herring Blake. Little, Brown Books for Young Readers, 2019. (L)

Sunny finally got the heart transplant she's been needing for two years, so now she can do all the things she's longed to do. She's fallen out with her best friend, so this summer she's determined to find a new best friend and kiss a boy. But then Sunny meets Quinn, and she's no longer sure if it's really a boy she wants to kiss after all.

Awards and Honors
- Starred reviews: *Booklist, Kirkus Reviews, School Library Journal*

Conversation Starters
1. Who would you include in your family, even if they aren't related to you, and why?
2. What would you do if you were able to?

The Mysterious Disappearance of Aidan S. (as Told to His Brother) by David Levithan. Random House Children's Books, 2021. (G)

One night, Aidan disappears. No one knows where he went, not even his brother, Lucas. Police are called and homes and neighborhoods are searched, but days go by without a sign. Then, as suddenly as he disappeared, Aidan comes back six nights later in his pajamas like nothing happened. For days he would tell no one where he went, but finally, he tells Lucas one night in the room they share. His story is impossible to believe, but Lucas helps his brother make up a plausible story to tell the police.

Awards and Honors
- Starred reviews: *Booklist, Publishers Weekly*

Conversation Starters
1. Do you ever feel like you don't belong where you are?
2. What is your special place in your home? Or elsewhere?

Nikhil Out Loud by Maulik Pancholy. Balzer + Bray, 2022. (G)

Nikhil voices the main character of a popular animated series, but when his grandfather becomes ill, he and his mom move from California to Ohio. It's a scary transition, and making friends at a new school, finding a new recording studio to keep up with episodes, and dealing with puberty, voice changes, and coming out as gay put a lot of pressure on Nikhil.

Awards and Honors
- Starred review: *Kirkus Reviews*

Conversation Starters
1. If you could voice any animated character, who would it be?
2. Is there something you do which is all that most people know you for? What might it like if that thing changes?

Obie Is Man Enough by Schuyler Bailar. Crown Books for Young Readers, 2021. (T)

Even after working endlessly to be the best on the swim team, when Obie comes out as trans to his swim coach, he's cut from the team. His best friend won't stick up for him, and his other good friend, who happens to be the son of his now-ex coach, has started bullying him. It gets so bad that Clyde attacks Obie in the school bathroom. Obie ends up needing stitches and has to stay out of the pool for two weeks, seriously endangering his chances of making it to Junior Olympics.

Conversation Starters
1. How does Obie deal with his intersectional identities?
2. How are LGBTQIA+ athletes treated?

The One Who Loves You the Most by medina. Levine Querido, 2022. (Q, P, I, T, L, Nonbinary, A)

Gabriela has a hard time figuring out how to be authentic, and of course that's the essay topic for English class. They're a transracial adoptee, their mom has depression, and ever since the big P (puberty), they don't fit into their own body. But soon they meet Héctor and Abbie, and actually talk to their crush, Maya, and learn about different LGBTQIA+ identities. Eventually, Gabriela finds the words that fit just right.

Awards and Honors
• Rainbow Book List, 2023

Conversation Starters
1. In what ways do you struggle to fit in?
2. Who did you expect to be the person who loves Gabriela the most, just from the title?

Rick by Alex Gino. Scholastic Press, 2020. (A, Q)

Rick does not like confrontation. It's easy to go along with his friend and dad when they tell sexist jokes or bully others. But when he gets to middle school, he begins to see the great variety of students and decides he needs to break ties with Jeff, his friend since second grade. While learning about all the clubs offered, he notices one called the Rainbow Spectrum club. This club gives him the friends and confidence to tell his father that he is unsure of his gender leanings.

Awards and Honors
• Starred reviews: *Booklist, Kirkus Reviews, Publishers Weekly, School Library Journal*

Conversation Starters

1. What happens when you follow along and do what a friend does, even if you disagree with it? How does it make you feel?
2. Have you ever had an interest you didn't share with anyone? Did you go ahead and follow it?

||||||||||||||||||||||

Authors Speak Out
Alex Gino

I can only imagine who I would be now if I had seen any sort of positive representation of transgender people in the many, many books I read growing up. If I can help kids see themselves now, I'm going to take that opportunity. . . . If you are a librarian, teacher, or other community member, you are working with LGBTQIA+ youth, whether you know it or not. . . . Providing support does not change who young people are, but young people who receive support have significantly higher mental health than those who do not.

Riley Reynolds Crushes Costume Day by Jay Albee. Capstone, 2022.

Riley Reynolds Rocks the Park by Jay Albee. Capstone, 2022.

Riley Reynolds Slays the Play by Jay Albee. Capstone, 2022.

Riley Reynolds Glitterfies the Gala by Jay Albee. Capstone, 2022. **(Nonbinary [all four titles])**

Riley is a nonbinary fourth grader, and this week their class is working on outfits for Costume Day. Riley is great at offering suggestions to their friends, and with a little help from neighborhood adults, everyone makes costumes that they love to wear.

Riley and friends bring tulip bulbs to a neighbor and play in the park.

Riley helps their class prepare for the class play.

Riley and friends raise money to fix the elevator at the library.

Awards and Honors
- Rainbow Book List, 2023 (all four titles)

Conversation Starters
1. Which character do you like best?
2. As you have read these books, what characteristics do you see being portrayed by the characters?
3. What skills—communication, sharing, compromise, or other—do you see at work in these books?
4. What project would you like to see Riley and their friends get involved in next?

Small Town Pride by Phil Stamper. HarperCollins, 2022. (G)

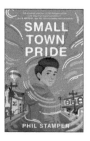

Jake lives in a really small town in Ohio, and when he came out as gay, his family and friends were very supportive. They're possibly too supportive. When his dad puts up a giant rainbow flag in their yard, Jake is embarrassed, and it only gets worse when the mayor starts getting complaints. The complaints spark worry that someone will try holding a Pride parade in town. But that doesn't seem like such a bad idea to Jake and his friends.

Awards and Honors
- Rainbow Book List, 2023

Conversation Starters
1. How can you show your friends you support them?
2. What experience have you had with overly supportive parents?

Spin with Me by Ami Polonsky. Farrar, Straus and Giroux Books for Young Readers, 2021. (Nonbinary)

Essie meets Ollie as she's counting down the days until she moves again. Ollie meets Essie as they're juggling advocacy and a crush on the new girl. Told in dual narratives, and from different time line directions, the story follows Ollie and Essie as they try to find a way through everything without spinning out of control.

Awards and Honors
- Starred review: *School Library Journal*

Conversation Starters
1. Have you ever had a crush on someone when one or both of you would be going away soon?
2. Which character's issue do you most connect with?

Too Bright to See by Kyle Lukoff. Dial Books, 2021. (T)

Bug doesn't want to think about preparing for middle school the way Moira does; Bug's tired of trying so hard to figure out how to be a girl. And who has time for that anyway when Bug's house seems to be haunted?

Awards and Honors
- Starred reviews: *Booklist, Kirkus Reviews, Publishers Weekly, School Library Journal*
- Stonewall Book Award–Mike Morgan and Larry Romans Children's Literature Award, 2022
- National Book Award for Young People's Literature finalist, 2021
- Newbery Honor Book, 2022

Conversation Starters
1. Are ghosts real?
2. Can a house be haunted by things other than ghosts?

Zenobia July by Lisa Bunker. Viking Books for Young Readers, 2019. (T, L)

Zenobia has a whole lot of new in her life: a new school, new friends, a new place to live with her lesbian aunts, and a new opportunity finally to live publicly as a girl. When someone posts hateful Islamophobic and transphobic memes on the school website, Zenobia knows her coding skills from her old life could help her catch the culprit, and suddenly she has new decisions to make: Whom can she trust? And is catching the hacker worth the attention and risk?

Conversation Starters
1. What's something you're really good at?
2. Have you ever struggled at times with feeling that people in your family don't understand you?

ACTIVITIES, PROJECTS, AND PROGRAMS FOR MIDDLE GRADE READERS

Perler Bead Pride Flag

Make pride flags or designs using pride flag colors. Perler beads are fairly inexpensive, and square bead boards are easy to source from craft stores. Make sure you have an iron (and patience) to fuse the designs together, but this activity provides kids with boundless freedom to create their own designs.

Bead Lizards

Bead lizards[1] are relatively easy to make using beads (maybe leftover perler beads from the previous activity), string/thread, and a jump ring if they'll become keychains. They can be done in pride flag colors by dividing the number of rows by colors in the pride flag; for example, four-color pride flags have rows one through four in the first color, rows five through eight in the second color, rows nine through twelve in the third color, and rows thirteen through sixteen in the fourth color; the Philadelphia pride flag has two rows of each color.

FIGURE 3.2
Pride flag bead lizard

Comic Writing Workshop

For those youth who enjoy reading comics and graphic novels, this is an opportunity for them to create their own. This may take a series of sessions to complete.

- They will first write their story idea.
- They then break it down into chunks that each can be represented in a panel box.
- They finally illustrate this story and even include some text.
- Host an author event to showcase the completed comics.

FIGURE 3.1

Perler bead pride flag

Design a Roller Coaster

Dalia from *Almost Flying* sure loves a roller coaster. Invite interested youth to design and create a roller coaster. Provide a variety of materials, such as construction paper, the cardboard tubes from paper towel rolls and toilet paper rolls, craft sticks, masking tape, and anything else you may have. Once the coasters are complete, provide youth with marbles to test to see which roller coasters have a successful design.

Plan a Road Trip

Youth today do not know the joy of physically plotting a road trip without using Waze, MapQuest, or Google Maps! After a group reads *Almost Flying,* challenge them to plot out a road trip to another destination. Provide resources like maps from AAA, travel guide books, paper and pencils, and calculators. They will select a location for their travels, and using the resources provided, they will calculate the route, the distance, any stops along the way, and potential necessary overnight stopping points. Then they can draw their maps, including fun stops, and make a playlist of songs. They may even want to draw up a snack list for the car trip!

WRAP-UP

As you can see from this chapter, a common theme of these books for middle grade readers is emerging identity. From Obie in *Obie Is Man Enough* to Bug in *Too Bright to See* and Gabriela in *The One Who Loves You the Most,* characters strive in a variety of ways, in various settings, and under a multitude of circumstances to understand themselves and their sexuality and gender identity. At the same time, these very characters hold close ties to family, still craving their love and support. The need for acceptance and understanding, from themselves, family members, and peers, is of utmost importance during this stage of children's development.

NOTE

1. Adapted from "Take and Make: Beaded Lizard Keychain," Fondulac District Library (East Peoria, IL), August 17, 2020, https://fondulaclibrary.org/2020/08/17/take-make-beaded-lizard-keychain/.

Books and Conversation for Younger Teens

A s LGBTQIA+ literature for children and teens expands, title selection becomes more difficult, but there are a few key parts we should look for, to make sure they are included. Teens need books with queer-normative settings, where LGBTQIA+ identities are normal and accepted, as in *The Heartbreak Bakery* (annotated in chapter 5). They need to see a variety of family structures, with combinations of queer kids and parents and families, both biological and found, like those in *Galaxy: The Prettiest Star*, *I Will Be Okay*, and *Middletown*. They need normalized queer relationships, and they need books that show LGBTQIA+ characters with self-confidence, like Kaia and Maren in *Shatter the Sky*.

|||||||||||||||||||||||||

Start Small
The First Younger Teen Books to Add to Your Collection

- *Cinderella Is Dead* by Kalynn Bayron
- *A Quick and Easy Guide to They/Them Pronouns* by Archie Bongiovanni and Tristan Jimerson
- *Felix Ever After* by Kacen Callender

||||||||||||||||||||||

Authors Speak Out
e. E. Charlton-Trujillo

The young people in your classrooms, libraries, afterschool programs, and other gatherings are a vibrant part of your community. They need your support to feel safe as their authentic selves. Offer them a place in conversations, organizations, and activities where their voices can be heard. To better celebrate them, gather resources from groups such as GLSEN, the Trevor Project, the Human Rights Campaign, or your local LGBTQIA+ support center. Learn about the ever-evolving lexicon that young people use in how they identify. Be fearless in checking your own biases as you do, and always remember these are kids—kids who need your compassion and understanding to better help them feel they can belong.

TRENDS IN LGBTQIA+ TEEN AND YA BOOKS

Young adult literature is moving away from books that focus solely on white gay boys and toward more intersectional identities (race, class, disability, etc.) and varied queer identities (bisexual, pansexual, asexual, transgender, nonbinary, etc.), and those identities are becoming more normalized and not a problem or an obstacle. We've gone from older titles like *Annie on My Mind* and *Rainbow Boys* to newer titles such as *Felix Ever After* and *Pet*. The diversity of queer identities represented in our selections is shown in figure 4.1.

SPECIAL FOCUS: MENTAL HEALTH

Many teens struggle with mental health issues, and LGBTQIA+ teens are more likely to be affected. Frequently, characters in LGBTQIA+ YA books deal with anxiety and depression, like the main character in *Moonflower* (annotated in chapter 3) and Kyra in *Before I Let Go*. Queer teens also frequently deal with being autistic, like Nick in *Hell Followed with Us* (annotated in chapter 5) and having ADHD (attention-deficit/hyperactivity disorder) and other neurodivergencies, like Bastián and Lore in *Lakelore* (annotated

FIGURE 4.1

Representation by type, number of teen and young adult books

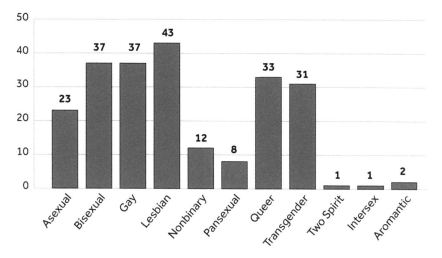

in chapter 5). Laura Dattaro, writing for *Spectrum* in 2020, reported on a study which noted that "people who do not identify with the sex they were assigned at birth are three to six times as likely to be autistic as cisgender people are."[1] These results were not just from one study, but "an analysis of five unrelated databases that all include information about autism, mental health and gender"[2] and corroborate anecdotal evidence we've seen in our communities.

According to the Trevor Project's *National Survey on LGBTQ Youth Mental Health 2021*, "42% of LGBTQ youth seriously considered attempting suicide in the past year, including more than half of transgender and nonbinary youth." Additionally, "94% of LGBTQ youth reported that recent politics negatively impacted their mental health." However, they go on to say that "LGBTQ youth who had access to spaces that affirmed their sexual orientation and gender identity reported lower rates of attempting suicide" than those who did not, and that "transgender and nonbinary youth who reported having pronouns respected by all of the people they lived with attempted suicide at half the rate of those who did not have their pronouns respected by anyone with whom they lived."[3] In an update in 2022, the rates had climbed to 45 percent of LGBTQ youth seriously considering attempting suicide, and in the wake of anti-transgender legislation affecting transgender and nonbinary youth, 93 percent worrying about state or local laws denying gender-affirming care, 91 percent worrying about bathroom access, and 83 percent worrying about sports inclusion.[4]

YOUNGER TEEN BOOKS THAT CAN BE USED IN OTHER DISPLAYS

Black History Month

Bitter	*Nothing Burns as Bright as You*
Felix Ever After	*Off the Record*
How to Be Remy Cameron	*Pet*
Little and Lion	*Rise to the Sun*

Hispanic Heritage Month

Café Con Lychee	*The Lesbiana's Guide to Catholic School*
I Will Be Okay	

Asian American and Pacific Islander Month

Café Con Lychee	*I'll Be the One*
Flip the Script	*Last Night at the Telegraph Club*
Hani and Ishu's Guide to Fake Dating	*The Magic Fish*
The Henna Wars	*Summer Bird Blue*

Valentine's Day/Romance

The Falling in Love Montage	*Hani and Ishu's Guide to Fake Dating*

St. Patrick's Day/Irish

The Falling in Love Montage	*The Henna Wars*
Hani and Ishu's Guide to Fake Dating	*Witches of Ash and Ruin*

Summer

The Girl from the Sea

Autism Acceptance Month

A Million Quiet Revolutions

FANTASY

Across the Green Grass Fields by Seanan McGuire. Tor, 2021. (I)

When Reagan tells her best friend, Laurel, that she's just found out that she's intersex, Laurel freaks out and calls Reagan a boy, so Reagan runs out of school and through the woods to get back to her house. But halfway home, she comes across two trees that have somehow grown together at the top, looking vaguely like a doorway, and the branches inexplicably spell out "Be Sure." Reagan's sure of nothing but ventures through and ends up not at her house, but in a world where centaurs are real, unicorns are simple herd animals, and a human turning up in the Hooflands means that something bad is about to happen.

Awards and Honors
- Starred reviews: *Library Reads*, *Publishers Weekly*
- Hugo Award for Best Novella nominee, 2022

Conversation Starters
1. Do you have any interests that your friends might think aren't suited to your gender?
2. *Across the Green Grass Fields* is a very short book. What do you think happens to Reagan after taking the portal back to her own world?

Cinderella Is Dead by Kalynn Bayron. Bloomsbury, 2020. (L)

Every year girls are required to attend the Prince's ball, keeping up the tradition from Cinderella. If a man does not pick them at the ball, they are never heard from again. When Sophia decides she'd rather marry her best friend, Erin, than be an object to be picked by some man she doesn't know, she's forced to flee and, later, confront the awful truth plaguing the kingdom.

Awards and Honors
- Starred review: *Booklist*
- Cybils Award nominee, 2020

- Book Shimmy Award, 2020
- Books Are My Bag Readers Award, YA Fiction, 2020
- CILIP Carnegie Medal nominee, 2020
- Wordery Children's Book of the Year, 2020
- Goodreads Choice Award, Young Adult Fantasy and Science Fiction nominee, 2020
- YALSA Amazing Audiobooks for Young Adults selection, 2022

Conversation Starters
1. Arranged marriages can be common in historical fiction and fantasy. How does the situation in *Cinderella Is Dead* differ?
2. How does *Cinderella Is Dead* subvert popular folktale tropes like the fairy godmother and the prince's ball, and what effect does that subversion have?

The Dark Tide by Alicia Jasinska. Sourcebooks Fire, 2020. (B)

Lina wants to save her brother from being this year's sacrifice to the witch queen, so she convinces Thomas, her friend and crush, to help her because he successfully escaped once. Queen Eva is determined to avoid her sister's mistake of sacrificing herself to save a boy. When Thomas is picked, Lina offers herself in exchange, and she and Eva find out neither is what the other expected while they wait for the eclipse and sacrifice.

Awards and Honors
- Starred reviews: *Booklist, School Library Journal*

Conversation Starters
1. What would it take to sacrifice yourself for a cause?
2. Was Lina willing to risk her entire island city just to save her brother?

Girl, Serpent, Thorn by Melissa Bashardoust. Flatiron Books, 2020. (B)

Soraya has spent her life away from others, a poison to anyone she touches or who touches her. She's safe only in her gardens. Her twin brother's wedding brings visitors, and Soraya is given the choice either to ask the demon in the dungeon about her curse or to spend time with a new young man who is unafraid of her power.

Awards and Honors
- Starred reviews: *Booklist, School Library Journal*
- Goodreads Choice Award, Young Adult Fantasy and Science Fiction nominee, 2020

Conversation Starters
1. How would you spend your time if you had to spend your life alone?
2. Would you allow anyone to risk their safety to keep you company?

Scavenge the Stars by Tara Sim. Little, Brown Books for Young Readers, 2021. (B)

Amaya knows she shouldn't have rescued a stranger from drowning. Because she did, she now owes even more time on the ship that she's forced to work on. But when the stranger gives her a chance at a new life and a chance at revenge on those who destroyed her family, it's hard to say no.

Conversation Starters
1. Have you ever impulsively done something that ended with you paying the price? Would you do it again, or is there another way to succeed in this gesture?
2. How far would you go for revenge?

Shatter the Sky by Rebecca Kim Wells. Simon & Schuster, 2019. (B)

When Kaia is abducted by the empire, Maren sets off on a quest to steal a dragon, rescue her girlfriend, and save her way of life.

Awards and Honors
- New England Book Award finalist, 2019
- Bisexual Book Award for Speculative Fiction, 2019

Conversation Starters
1. A lot of YA books that feature romance include the beginnings of a relationship. In what ways was this book able to circumvent expectations by having the relationship already established?
2. How does Maren's sense of smell impact the writing and her character?

***These Witches Don't Burn* by Isabel Sterling. Razorbill, 2019. (L)**

***This Coven Won't Break* by Isabel Sterling. Razorbill, 2020. (L)**

In *These Witches Don't Burn*, Hannah's a witch in Salem, Massachusetts, trying to avoid her ex-girlfriend and fellow witch, Veronica, while working at the local metaphysical shop. When signs of dark magic show up around town, the coven is not convinced, so the exes are forced to team up, and Hannah just hopes the situation doesn't destroy her chances with the cute new girl in town, Morgan.

In *This Coven Won't Break*, Hannah and Morgan must stop the Witch Hunters before all of the witches lose their powers.

Conversation Starters
1. Queer teen witches are a microtrend. How does this duology compare to other books involving queer teen witches?
2. What life situations are the same and which are different because these girls are witches?

***Witches of Ash and Ruin* by E. Latimer. Little, Brown Books for Young Readers, 2020. (B)**

After everything Dayna's been through, she longs to become a full witch in her coven. Unfortunately, right before that's supposed to happen, another coven comes to town, a witch turns up dead with all of the trademarks of a notorious serial killer, and the ceremony that should go smoothly goes very, very wrong.

Conversation Starters
1. In this highly charged adventure, what part did you like best and why?
2. Which intrigued you more, the witchy business or the romance?

GRAPHIC NONFICTION

***How to Be Ace: A Memoir of Growing Up Asexual* by Rebecca Burgess. Jessica Kingsley Publishers, 2020. (A)**

Rebecca Burgess details in graphic-memoir form the experience of growing up asexual in a sexualized world.

Awards and Honors
- Prism Award for Small/Midsize Press nominee, 2021

Conversation Starters
1. What did you learn from studying the advertisements about body image?
2. What are your thoughts about the amount of subtle sexualization you now notice in magazines and books?

A Quick and Easy Guide to Asexuality by Molly Muldoon, illustrated by Will Hernandez. Limerence Press, 2022. (A)

Asexuality is often misunderstood, if it is known at all, and there are a lot of variations in ways to be asexual. Molly Muldoon and Will Hernandez attempt to show what asexuality really is, and what it's like to be asexual.

Awards and Honors
- Over the Rainbow Short List, 2023
- Rainbow Book List, 2023

Conversation Starters
1. What misconceptions did you have about asexuality before reading this book?
2. Now that you are aware of asexuality, what has changed for you as you read and watch movies?

A Quick and Easy Guide to They/Them Pronouns by Archie Bongiovanni and Tristan Jimerson. Oni Press, 2018. (T, Nonbinary)

Two comics artists join forces to explain what pronouns are, why it's important to get someone's pronouns right, and what to do if you mess up.

Awards and Honors
- Starred review: *School Library Journal*
- VLA Graphic Novel Diversity Award, Youth Category Honor Book, 2018

Conversation Starters
1. What pronouns do you use?
2. Do you know anybody who uses pronouns other than *he* or *she*?

GRAPHIC NOVELS

Across a Field of Starlight **by Blue Delliquanti. Random House Graphic, 2022. (T, Nonbinary)**

Two teens on opposite sides of a galactic war, one raised in a culture of peace and one from a militaristic resistance movement, keep in contact when they can after they accidentally meet as kids on a neutral planet. They have to be careful that no one finds out about their friendship, or lives would certainly be at stake.

Awards and Honors
- Rainbow Book List, 2023

Conversation Starters
1. What are some similarities and differences between this book and *Romeo and Juliet*?
2. What aspects of a galactic war impact this story?

Belle of the Ball **by Mari Costa. First Second, 2023. (L)**

Hawkins has a crush on Regina, but Regina's already dating Chloe. In an effort to gain Regina's favor, Hawkins offers to tutor Chloe.

Conversation Starters
1. Are you mostly the same person you were when you were younger, or are you different? How?
2. What is different about this classic love triangle?

Doughnuts and Doom **by Balazs Lorinczi. Top Shelf, 2022. (L)**

A struggling witch accidentally curses the lead singer in her favorite local band at the doughnut shop. Magic and sparks fly.

Conversation Starters
1. What was the most life-changing doughnut you've ever eaten?
2. What made you select a graphic rom-com today?

Flamer by Mike Curato. Henry Holt Books for Young Readers, 2020. (G)

Aiden can't possibly be gay. Everybody's always told him bad things about people who are gay. But it's summer, Aiden's at camp, everybody's going through puberty, and he just can't get another boy out of his head.

Awards and Honors
- Starred reviews: *Booklist*, *Horn Book*, *Kirkus Reviews*
- Lambda Literary Award for LGBTQ Young Adult, 2021

Conversation Starters
1. Aiden deals with internalized homophobia. What internalized biases do you struggle with?
2. How would you deal with "the heart wants what the heart wants" in this situation?

Galaxy: The Prettiest Star by Jadzia Axelrod. DC Comics, 2022. (T)

Taylor seems perfectly normal, with good grades and a place on the basketball team, except that version of Taylor isn't the real one. Taylor is really an alien princess, in exile from an intergalactic war and hiding on Earth as a human boy. When Taylor finds a way to at least temporarily change back, masquerading as a human boy seems less and less appealing.

Awards and Honors
- Starred review: *Publishers Weekly*
- Rainbow Book List, 2023

Conversation Starters
1. How does the main character's disguise as a human reflect or portray transness?
2. How would this story change if Taylor hid out on Earth as a girl?

The Girl from the Sea by Molly Knox Ostertag. Graphix, 2021. (L)

Morgan can't wait to get away from her small island and all of the people who think they know her but don't know her secrets. When she almost drowns one night, she's saved by a girl named Keltie, who's also hiding a few things. As their connection grows, secrets have a way of coming out.

Awards and Honors
- Starred reviews: *Publishers Weekly, School Library Journal*
- Goodreads Choice Award, Graphic Novels and Comics nominee, 2021
- Great Graphic Novels for Teens Top Ten, 2022
- Top Ten Quick Picks for Reluctant Young Adult Readers, 2022
- Rainbow Book List Top Ten for Teen Readers, 2022

Conversation Starters
1. How much do you know about selkie mythology?
2. Does home have a way of pulling you back in, even when you want to get out?

Heartstopper #1 by Alice Oseman. Graphix, 2020. (G)
Heartstopper #2 by Alice Oseman. Graphix, 2020. (G)
Heartstopper #3 by Alice Oseman. Graphix, 2021. (G)
Heartstopper#4 by Alice Oseman. Graphix, 2022. (G)

Charlie Spring was outed and bullied at his British grammar school, but life is starting to get a little better. When he meets Nick Nelson, star of the school's rugby team, they quickly become friends, and soon Charlie develops a massive crush on Nick, despite their differences. This webcomic/graphic novel series was also the basis for a Netflix series.

Awards and Honors
- Starred review, *Heartstopper #2*: *Kirkus Reviews*
- *Heartstopper #2*: Goodreads Choice Award, Graphic Novels and Comics nominee, 2019
- *Heartstopper #3*: Goodreads Choice Award, Graphic Novels and Comics, 2020

Conversation Starters

1. In *Heartstopper #4*, Charlie and Nick have become a couple. How do the issues of an eating disorder and mental health impact this budding love affair?
2. Do you have a friend you suspect has an eating disorder? How can you support them?

The Magic Fish **by Trung Le Nguyen. Random House Graphic, 2020. (G)**

Tien doesn't have the language to tell his parents that he's gay. Literally. His parents struggle with learning English, and he doesn't know how to explain it in Vietnamese. He also doesn't want to lose the magic of reading stories from the library together. He finds a way to stitch parts of the story together, hoping that will explain things.

Awards and Honors

- Starred reviews: *Booklist, Bulletin of the Center for Children's Books, Horn Book, Kirkus Reviews, Publishers Weekly*
- Goodreads Choice Award, Graphic Novels and Comics nominee, 2020
- British Fantasy Award, Best Comic/Graphic Novel nominee, 2021
- Amelia Elizabeth Walden Award nominee, 2022

Conversation Starters

1. What folktales can you use to explain situations to your family?
2. In what ways does the author/illustrator use color within the folktales?

HISTORICAL FICTION

Last Night at the Telegraph Club **by Malinda Lo. Dutton Books, 2021. (L)**

In 1950s San Francisco, Chinese American Lily Hu is beginning to realize that something about her is different, but she hasn't yet been able to put words to it. When she accidentally drops a clipped ad for a male impersonator at a lesbian club in front of her white friend Kath, she does not expect Kath's offer to attend with her but hesitantly accepts. As her individual world expands, her family life closes in on her, and Lily faces the difficult situation of being caught between who her family expects her to be and who she knows she is.

Awards and Honors
- Starred reviews: *Booklist, Bulletin of the Center for Children's Books, Kirkus Reviews, Publishers Weekly*
- National Book Award for Young People's Literature, 2021
- *Los Angeles Times* Book Prize for Young Adult Literature nominee, 2021
- Goodreads Choice Award, Young Adult Fiction nominee, 2021
- Michael L. Printz Award nominee, 2022
- Asian/Pacific American Award for Literature, 2022
- Walter Dean Myers Award, Teen nominee, 2022
- Stonewall Book Award–Mike Morgan and Larry Romans Children's Literature Award, 2022

Conversation Starters
1. Both Lily's Chinese heritage and her lesbian identity make her stand out. What instances of racism and homophobia does she face, and who perpetrates them?
2. What was new to you about the historical and cultural context of the novel?

NONFICTION

The 57 Bus by Dashka Slater. Farrar, Straus, and Giroux Books for Young Readers, 2017. (T, Nonbinary, A)

Sasha is napping on the bus on their way home from school when Richard's friends goad him into putting a lighter to Sasha's skirt. They don't know that Sasha is agender or has Asperger's.[5] They see someone who they think is a boy wearing a skirt, and they think it will be funny. None of them think about the consequences. But in the short time where they intersect on that bus route, their lives and futures change.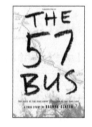

What could be a simple victim-villain dynamic instead unfolds through the long lines of privilege and racism, poverty and wealth, and peer pressure and individuality, and explores the concepts of restorative justice in a world where it is all too easy to allow a school-to-prison pipeline to exist.

Awards and Honors
- Starred reviews: *Kirkus Reviews, Publishers Weekly, School Library Journal*
- California Book Award for Young Adult Gold, 2017
- *Los Angeles Times* Book Prize for Young Adult Literature nominee, 2017
- *Boston Globe*–Horn Book Award, Nonfiction nominee, 2018
- Stonewall Award–Mike Morgan and Larry Romans Children's Literature Award, 2018
- YALSA Award for Excellence in Nonfiction for Young Adults finalist, 201
- Rhode Island Teen Book Award nominee, 2019
- Lincoln Award nominee, 2020
- Evergreen Teen Book Award, High School nominee, 2020

Conversation Starters
1. Have you ever done something without thinking it through and had it get much bigger than you'd planned?
2. Should restorative justice be an option for criminal cases, or should it be confined to school disagreements?

Growing Up Trans, edited by Dr. Lindsay Herriot and Kate Fry. Orca, 2021. (T)

Growing Up Trans is a collection of poems, essays, and art from transgender kids in Canada, along with information, resources, and discussion questions from subject specialists.

Conversation Starters
1. How do you see yourself, and how does that compare to how other people see you?
2. Are the experiences of the teens in *Growing Up Trans* like your own experiences?

I Am Ace: Advice on Living Your Best Asexual Life by Cody Daigle-Orians. Jessica Kingsley Publishers, 2023. (A)

There are, so far, few nonfiction books for teens on the topic of asexuality. Cody Daigle-Orians translates his social media success as AceDadAdvice into giving, well, ace dad advice. *I Am Ace* covers what asexuality is (and isn't), types of asexuality, and how to talk to people about asexuality, relationships, and asexuality in the wider queer community.

Conversation Starters
1. What most surprised you about *I Am Ace*?
2. In the book, Cody talks about polyamory, which is also rarely talked about. Do you see any tension between asexuality and polyamory?

REALISTIC FICTION

Aces Wild by Amanda DeWitt. Peachtree Teen, 2022. (A)

What happens when you mix *Ocean's 11* with Arthurian mythology and populate the heist team with a group of asexual teens meeting in person for the first time? When Jack Shannon's mom is arrested and her casino is under threat of buyout by a fellow casino owner with mafia ties, Jack does the only thing he can think of to save his mom, the casino, and his family: he flies out his online asexual friend group under the guise of a youth conference, and they plan a heist to expose the rival casino owner.

Conversation Starters
1. How does *Aces Wild* show the spectrum of asexual identities?
2. What is the wildest plan you've ever concocted with your friends?

At the End of Everything by Marieke Nijkamp. Sourcebooks Fire, 2022. (A, Q, Nonbinary)

A group of teens live in a juvenile treatment center, cut off from most people and society. One day, the guards start acting strangely, and soon none of them show up at all. The kids are forced to find a way to free themselves and take care of their needs. But resources are slim, and they start hearing that there is a dangerous, highly infectious disease making its way through the world, and no one is allowed to travel without a permit.

Conversation Starters

1. The teens at Hope Juvenile Treatment Center are abandoned first by their families, and then again by the guards. How do these abandonments affect them?
2. Most books that center on disaster scenarios use natural disasters or war as their spark. This book uses an infectious disease and was published during the COVID-19 pandemic. Does it elicit any recognition of differing levels of privilege during such scenarios?

Be Dazzled by Ryan La Sala. Sourcebooks Fire, 2021. (G)

Raffy is determined to win a cosplay crafting competition at an upcoming convention. Unfortunately, his ex, Luca, has the same idea. When they're forced to team up in the competition, can they put the past behind them and make it work, or will all of their hard work go up in glitter?

Awards and Honors
- Starred review: *Publishers Weekly*
- Audie Award for Best Young Adult, 2022

Conversation Starters

1. If you were designing a cosplay, what character/fandom would you choose?
2. How does cosplay serve as a vehicle to test out identities?

Before I Let Go by Marieke Nijkamp. Sourcebooks Fire, 2018. (P, A)

Corey is from a small town in Alaska, and after moving away, she's back to find out what happened to her best friend, Kyra, who died just days before. Something strange is going on in Lost Creek, and it doesn't seem like the town Corey left.

Awards and Honors
- Starred review: *Booklist*

Conversation Starters

1. Have you ever lost touch with a friend? What happened?
2. Could Corey have done more for Kyra?

Between Perfect and Real by Ray Stoeve. Henry N. Abrams, 2021. (T)

Everyone thinks Dean's a lesbian, but he knows he's trans. The school theater director thinks casting an untraditional Romeo makes the school play edgy, but it just makes Dean long even more to be seen, not as a lesbian, but as a trans guy.

Awards and Honors
- Starred review: *Booklist*

Conversation Starters
1. Dean's girlfriend has difficulties when he comes out as trans. How do they each deal with their feelings?
2. What are some of the results when a story is gender bent? And is there ultimately a difference when the changes are made for a reason other than just to be edgy?

Café Con Lychee by Emery Lee. Quill Tree Books, 2022. (G)

Two cafés, both alike in dignity, in fair Vermont where we lay our scene. Theo and Gabi both work for their parents' competing restaurants, Theo's Asian American café and Gabi's Puerto Rican bakery. Gabi is also envious that Theo is able to be out while he is stuck in the closet. But when a new fusion café opens in town, catering to all things Instagramable, Theo and Gabi have no choice but to team up if they want to save their parents' businesses.

Awards and Honors
- Rainbow Book List, 2023

Conversation Starters
1. The rivalry between Theo's and Gabi's parents at the beginning is fairly intense. What parallels can you find with famous rivalries, either historical or fictional?
2. How does the issue of Gabi still being in the closet impact this story?

Deposing Nathan by Zack Smedley. Page Street Publishing, 2019. (B)

Through flashbacks and deposition testimony, Nathan tells the story of how he met Cam, how they became close, and just how he got stabbed in the stomach.

Awards and Honors
- Starred review: *Kirkus Reviews*
- Lambda Literary Award finalist, 2019
- Bisexual Book Award for Teen/Young Adult Fiction, 2019

Conversation Starters
1. Nathan struggles with both religion and sexuality. Does this parallel or inform how he tells his side of the story?
2. Nathan and Cam deal with a lot of homophobia, both internal and external. How does that play out with the abuse?

The Falling in Love Montage by Ciara Smyth. HarperTeen, 2020. (L)

Saoirse isn't exactly a romantic, and she certainly isn't looking for a relationship, because there's a chance she'll develop the same type of early-onset dementia that's affecting her mother. Then she meets Ruby, who suggests that they do all the rom-com montage clichés, but they break up at the end of summer.

Awards and Honors
- Starred review: *Publishers Weekly*
- Best Fiction for Young Adults, 2021

Conversation Starters
1. What rom-com montage cliché would you most want to do with someone?
2. Do you think you'd have an easy time breaking off a relationship at the end of summer like Saoirse and Ruby plan to?

Felix Ever After by Kacen Callender. Balzer + Bray, 2020. (T, Q)

Felix is worried that he'll never find love as a queer Black trans person. It gets worse when someone begins sending and posting transphobic messages along with pictures of Felix pretransition and his deadname. But a plan for revenge ends up going in an entirely different direction than Felix ever imagined.

Awards and Honors
- Starred reviews: *Booklist, Publishers Weekly, School Library Journal*
- Goodreads Choice Award, Young Adult Fiction nominee, 2020

Conversation Starters
1. How does Felix evolve?
2. Do you think that Felix's story is a love story? If not, what kind of story do you think it is?

Flip the Script by Lyla Lee. Katherine Tegen Books, 2022. (B)

Hana loves K-dramas, and now she's been cast in a new series. To keep the buzz on the show going, the producers decide that she and her on-screen love interest should take things off-screen as well, or at least fake it. But then her fake boyfriend is starting to act like he's really falling for her, and when the writers add a rival for her on-screen boyfriend's affections, romance and drama start to heat up.

Awards and Honors
- Rainbow Book List, 2023

Conversation Starters
1. In what ways does this book flip the script on love triangles in YA books?
2. How do you think Hana should handle this fake love-interest story? How about when they add the rival interest?

The Ghosts We Keep by Mason Deaver. PUSH, 2021. (T, Nonbinary)

Liam's older brother is killed in a hit-and-run accident, and they don't know how to connect with their best friends anymore. The only person Liam can think of who might share their level of grief is their brother Ethan's best friend, Marcus. Soon Liam discovers that Ethan might have had more secrets than even Liam knew.

Awards and Honors
• Starred review: *Booklist*

Conversation Starters
1. Can we ever really know someone?
2. What would you do if you found out a secret that could change how someone is perceived?

Hani and Ishu's Guide to Fake Dating by Adiba Jaigirdar. Page Street Kids, 2021. (B)

Hani's friends don't believe that she's really bisexual because she's dated only guys. Feeling like she has to prove her sexuality, she panics and tells them that she's dating the only other Southeast Asian girl at her school, Ishu. Luckily, Ishu agrees to fake date Hani in return for help becoming Head Girl. But friends and feelings start getting in the way, and something has to give.

Awards and Honors
• Goodreads Choice Award, Young Adult Fiction nominee, 2021

Conversation Starters
1. Would you ever pretend to date someone? What would be a good reason?
2. Do you think someone can be bisexual if they've dated people of only one gender?

The Henna Wars by Adiba Jaigirdar. Page Street Kids, 2020. (L)

Nishat and Flávia's school holds a competition for students to choose and operate businesses, and they both decide to offer henna services. The trouble is, henna is a part of Nishat's culture but not Flávia's, so Nishat accuses her of appropriation. Amid the intrigue, the girls get to know each other a lot better, and competition forges an unexpected bond between the two.

Awards and Honors
- Starred review: *Kirkus Reviews*
- Goodreads Choice Award, Young Adult Fiction nominee, 2020

Conversation Starters
1. How well does *The Henna Wars* deal with the topic of appropriation?
2. When you adopt a new habit or outlet from another culture, do you wonder about the consequences of appropriation? Is there a difference between appropriation and appreciation?

Her Royal Highness by Rachel Hawkins. G. P. Putnam's Sons Books for Young Readers, 2018. (B, L)

After a relationship goes sour, Millie finds herself moving from life in Houston, Texas, to a boarding school in Scotland. While she's thrilled to be there, she is at odds with her roommate, Flora, who is acting like a princess. This is an enemies-to-lovers and a they-were-roommates story, with a dash of secret-royalty.

Conversation Starters
1. Would you move to a foreign country just to avoid someone?
2. How much research would you do before moving to a foreign country?

Here the Whole Time by Vitor Martins, translated by Larissa Helena. Scholastic Press, 2020. (G)

Felipe can't wait for school break; he's tired of the incessant teasing at school for being fat, and he can spend his time reading, binging shows, and watching YouTube. But then comes the best/worst news: the neighbor kid, Caio, who Felipe incidentally has a crush on, is going to be staying with Felipe for the next two weeks while his parents are on vacation.

Conversation Starters
1. What do you do if your parents put you in an uncomfortable position?
2. How do Felipe's thoughts about himself change by the end of this book?

How to Be Remy Cameron by Julian Winters. Duet, 2019. (G)

Remy thinks he knows who he is: he's Black, gay, and adopted. But when he's assigned to write about who he actually is, he doesn't really know what to say. In the course of trying to figure it out, he connects with a birth relative online who might have some answers, all while starting to crush on the new guy in his class.

Awards and Honors
• Starred review: *School Library Journal*

Conversation Starters
1. Do you know who you really are? Does anyone?
2. Which is more important to you, the family you're born into or the one you make?

I Will Be Okay by Bill Elenbark. Walrus Publishing, 2020. (G)

Mateo and Stick live down the street from each other, and although they're best friends, their lives couldn't be more different. Mateo's family is focused purely on his baseball prospects, despite his interests in other things, and Stick's family, with thirteen kids, is even more chaotic than Mateo's. When Mateo is injured, threatening his future playing baseball, and Stick loses his father, things fall apart. But just maybe, together they will be okay.

Conversation Starters
1. How do Mateo and Stick manage the expectations others have placed on them?
2. Does your family and your friend's family have similar goals for each of you? If not, does this challenge your friendship at times?

If I Can Give You That by Michael Gray Bulla. Quill Tree Books, 2023. (T, G, Q)

Trans boy Gael gets gently pushed by a friend into attending a group for queer teens. He has a lot going on in his life, between his depressed mother, estranged father, and a conservative school. But then he meets Declan, and he finds himself making more friends and having more people to count on, even as his mother's mental health worsens.

Conversation Starters
1. Have you ever gone to any type of support group? Was it helpful?
2. Do you believe the queer teen group will help Gael in dealing with his mother's mental health issues?

I'll Be the One by Lyla Lee. Katherine Tegan Books, 2020. (B)

Skye wants to be the first plus-sized K-pop star, and a reality TV competition might just give her that chance; but she'll have to get past "fatphobia," media scrutiny, and attraction to one of the other contestants to have a shot at winning.

Awards and Honors
- Starred reviews: *Kirkus Reviews*, *School Library Journal*

Conversation Starters
1. Skye does not hesitate to call out the unrealistic beauty standards not just in the United States, but in Korea. What unrealistic appearance standards have you experienced?
2. Late in the book Skye finds out that her mother also used to be fat, and that's why she's been so hard on Skye. Does that knowledge change your impression of Skye's mom?

Just Ash by Sol Santana. Carolrhoda Lab, 2021. (I)

Ash knew from a young age that he was intersex, but when he gets his period for the first time in the middle of soccer practice at age sixteen, everything shifts. He's a guy, but everyone sees him differently. His coach cuts him from the team, and his mom wants him to grow his hair out, wear makeup, and "try to be a girl," "try to be normal." It gets so bad that he runs away from home, to his sister's apartment in Boston.

Awards and Honors
- Starred review: *Booklist*
- Rainbow Book List Top Ten for Teen Readers, 2023

Conversation Starters
1. How does Ash see being intersex as being like the witches in Salem?
2. How do the people in Ash's life affirm his identity?

Late to the Party by Kelly Quindlen. Roaring Brook Press, 2020. (L)

Codi's never done the things that it seems like all of the other teenagers have done—crashed a party, kissed a girl, stayed out too late . . . but when she's talked into going to a party and accidentally finds cool kid Ricky kissing another guy, all that changes. Ricky decides to show her all the things she thinks she's missed out on in exchange for her not telling everybody about the kiss.

Conversation Starters
1. Are there stereotypical high school things that you worry you've missed out on? Do you feel pressure to do those things?
2. What do you think Cody learned from Ricky? Was there a lesson to be learned?

The Lesbiana's Guide to Catholic School by Sonora Reyes. Balzer + Bray, 2022. (L, B)

Yamilet has just moved to a new Catholic school after being outed by her now ex-best friend, and she's determined to not let anyone know she's gay, much less fall in love. Unfortunately, her plans might be quickly thwarted by an annoyingly perfect out girl named Bo.

Awards and Honors
- Pura Belpré Young Adult Author Honor Book, 2023
- William C. Morris Award finalist, 2023
- Rainbow Book List, 2023

Conversation Starters

1. One of the issues for Yamilet is that her father has been deported, so her mother is trying to raise Yamilet and her brother on her own. In what ways does Yamilet's father's absence impact her and how she and others view her sexuality?
2. How difficult do you think it would be to be a lesbian in a Catholic school as opposed to a public school?

Little and Lion by Brandy Colbert. Little, Brown Books for Young Readers, 2017 (B)

Suzette is back home in Los Angeles after attending a boarding school in New England, and while she's happy to be back where her family and crush are, her brother has been diagnosed as bipolar, and he needs a lot of help. Unfortunately, his mental health starts to spiral at the same time that Suzette realizes they're both falling for the same girl.

Awards and Honors

- Starred reviews: *Booklist*, *Bulletin of the Center for Children's Books*, *Kirkus Reviews*, *School Library Journal*
- Stonewall Book Award–Mike Morgan and Larry Romans Children's Literature Award, 2018

Conversation Starters

1. Could Suzette's bisexuality have been depicted without showing her crushing on both a boy and a girl?
2. Was there something that Suzette could have or should have done for her brother that she didn't do?

Look by Zan Romanoff. Dial Books, 2020. (L, B)

Lulu practically lives on social media, but after a video of her kissing another girl accidentally gets posted, her boyfriend dumps her, and the shiny life she shows off on Flash is revealed as completely faked. But then there's this girl, Cass, who invites her to hang out at a hotel that some young guy with a trust fund is having renovated to appeal to a new demographic, and it's fun for Lulu to hang out with Cass around the hotel. Unfortunately, while Lulu and Cass are falling for each other, the trust fund boy is taking pictures of the renovation process—and the two of them.

Awards and Honors
- Starred review: *Bulletin of the Center for Children's Books*

Conversation Starters
1. Who owns the rights to photographs? Can a photographer exhibit photographs of other people without their knowledge or consent?
2. How do these issues come into play online, especially in social media?

Love Is for Losers by Wibke Brueggemann. Farrar, Straus and Giroux Books for Young Readers, 2021. (L)

Phoebe hates the idea of falling in love. It's the worst, and she swears it off completely. Cue new girl Emma walking into her life, and all the things Phoebe thinks she knows become somewhat murkier.

Awards and Honors
- Starred review: *Publishers Weekly*

Conversation Starters
1. Have you ever decided to swear off the idea of falling in love? What happened?
2. Is there a good time to fall in love? Must it be by a certain age?

Middletown by Sarah Moon. Levine Querido, 2021. (Q)

Eli and her older sister, Anna, are close. They've had to be, with an absent dad and an alcoholic mom whose antics have gotten her forced into rehab. The girls have no desire to land in foster care, where they might be split up, so Anna pretends to be Eli's aunt and holds child services at bay for as long as she can. Unfortunately, Anna's habits of spending long periods of time with boys and staying out late make this tenuous plan even harder.

Awards and Honors
- Starred review: *Publishers Weekly*

Conversation Starters
1. Anna and Eli are let down time and time again by their mom. How well does Anna do as a surrogate, and should she have to make those choices?
2. Do you think this is a realistic plot? Why or why not?

A Million Quiet Revolutions by Robin Gow. Farrar, Straus and Giroux, 2022. (T)

Aaron and Oliver have been two of the very few out queer teens in their town, and certainly the only two trans guys. They share a deep bond, but when Aaron moves away, they start discovering records of American Revolutionary War soldiers who may have been, like them, both trans and in love.

Awards and Honors
- Starred review: *School Library Journal*
- Rainbow Book List, 2023

Conversation Starters
1. The queer community doesn't have a lot of queer elders. What are some factors that you think have contributed to that?
2. What have you done to maintain a bond with someone who moved away?

Nothing Burns as Bright as You by Ashley Woodfolk. Versify, 2022. (L)

Told in verse, this book follows two girls who were best friends, then romantic, then frayed, and then burned like the fire they start.

Awards and Honors
- Starred reviews: *Book Page, Booklist, Kirkus Reviews, Publishers Weekly, School Library Journal*
- Rainbow Book List Top Ten for Teen Readers, 2023

Conversation Starters

1. How would this story be different if it were written in prose instead of poetry?
2. What do you think about this entire book taking place in one day?

Off the Record by Camryn Garrett. Knopf Books for Young Readers, 2021. (B)

Josie wins a contest to follow a hot young actor on a press tour for his new movie about conversion therapy. She's excited for the opportunity, and to meet so many new people, until someone slips her an awful secret about sexual assault. Suddenly the celebrity profile she's supposed to write gets pushed back in favor of covering the increasingly messy truth of fame in Hollywood.

Awards and Honors

- Starred reviews: *Kirkus Reviews, Publishers Weekly, School Library Journal*
- Best Fiction for Young Adults, 2022

Conversation Starters

1. How does this book treat the topic of sexual assault compared to how the topic is covered in newspapers and magazines and/or online?
2. How would you handle this situation? Would you share the secret? Why or why not?

The One True Me and You by Remi K. England. Wednesday Books, 2022. (L, Nonbinary)

What happens when a Sherlock Holmes–themed convention takes place at the same hotel as a beauty pageant? A fanfic author competing for a spot in an anthology and a beauty pageant contestant hoping for a scholarship literally run into each other.

Conversation Starters
1. How far would you go for a scholarship?
2. What fandoms are you into? How much is queerness a part of that fandom?

___

The Prom: A Novel Based on the Hit Broadway Musical by Saundra Mitchell. Viking Books for Young Readers, 2019. (L)

The only thing Emma wants is to dance with her girlfriend Alyssa at prom, but the PTA in her small town is determined not to let them "ruin" prom for the rest of the students. Enter two slightly washed-up Broadway stars with their own agenda, pushing Emma and Alyssa to fight for what they want.

Conversation Starters
1. What does this book have to say about teenagers and their own agency, in regard to both Barry and Dee Dee as well as Alyssa's mother?
2. Do you think it would be hard to be in a relationship where one person is out and the other isn't?

___

Rise to the Sun by Leah Johnson. Scholastic Press, 2021. (Q)

Olivia wants one good concert weekend with her best friend before she has to go back to the reality of what caused her last breakup, and Toni has only a week before she starts college, so she's spending it at the music festival that gave her father his start.

Awards and Honors
• Starred review: *Publishers Weekly*

Conversation Starters
1. How do outside expectations of us influence the choices we make?
2. What do you think about a music festival as a book setting?

Sasha Masha by Agnes Borinsky. Farrar, Straus and Giroux Books for Young Readers, 2020. (T, Q)

Alex has never fit in anywhere. When he starts dating Tracy, he struggles with trying to be a good "boyfriend" and dreams of wearing dresses and lipstick. Maybe the problem isn't Alex being a good boyfriend. Maybe Alex is really Sasha.

Conversation Starters
1. Do you equate gender expression and gender performance with gender identity?
2. Is it difficult to figure out where you fit in?

She Drives Me Crazy by Kelly Quindlen. Roaring Brook Press, 2021. (L)

Scottie crashes her car into Irene's after blowing a basketball game against her ex, and of course both moms agree that the girls should carpool until Irene's car is fixed, even though the two are far from friends, or even friendly. But when Scottie figures out a way to get back at her awful ex, using this carpool arrangement to her advantage by pretending she and Irene are dating, she might just hit a few speed bumps and ignore a stop sign or two.

Awards and Honors
- Starred review: *Booklist*
- Goodreads Choice Award, Young Adult Fiction nominee, 2021
- Best Fiction for Young Adults, 2022

Conversation Starters
1. Fake dating is a common fiction trope. How well is it handled in *She Drives Me Crazy* as opposed to other books with the trope?
2. Do you think carpooling is a good answer to wrecked cars?

Ship It by Britta Lundin. Disney-Hyperion, 2018. (L, P, Q)

Claire is a capital-*F* Fan of the TV show *Demon Heart,* and her fanfiction is all centered on the two main characters getting together romantically. In an attempt to make her favorite slash pairing canon, she confronts the actors and producer at a convention. How far is she willing to go for her 'ship? Could it even work? And in her quest to increase queer representation, is she forgetting other marginalized groups? This is a book about fans and fandom, but not the cutesy, fun parts of fandom; this is the messy, dramatic pit-of-bad-decisions part of fandom.

Awards and Honors
- Starred review: *VOYA*

Conversation Starters
1. What fictional characters do you think should get together?
2. How far would you go to influence the plot of a TV or movie series?
3. Real-person fanfiction: fine or icky?

Summer Bird Blue by Akemi Dawn Bowman. Simon & Schuster Books for Young Readers, 2018. (A)

Rumi's world falls apart when her sister dies suddenly. To make things worse, her mother ships her off to live with an aunt in Hawaii. She struggles to navigate her grief and sense of abandonment with the help of her new neighbors, a teenage surfer and a taciturn eighty-year-old.

Awards and Honors
- Starred reviews: *Booklist, Kirkus Reviews, School Library Journal*

Conversation Starters
1. Music is a big part of Rumi's life. Is there a song that encapsulates who you are (at the moment, at least)?
2. What kind of trial and error have you had to go through to figure out who you are?

The Upside of Unrequited by Becky Albertalli. Balzer + Bray, 2017 (L)

Molly and Cassie's moms get engaged on the day the Supreme Court decides *Obergefell v. Hodges,* and while Molly's excited for her moms, she's feeling a little left out, especially when Cassie gets a new girlfriend. After crushing on boy after boy after boy, Molly thinks she'll never get a boyfriend. Enter Cassie's girlfriend's friend named Will and Molly's geeky new coworker, Reid.

Awards and Honors
- Starred review: *School Library Journal*
- Goodreads Choice Award, Young Adult Fiction nominee, 2017

Conversation Starters
1. Does Molly's weight factor into her self-esteem and anxiety?
2. What could Molly have done differently?

Wild and Crooked by Leah Thomas. Bloomsbury YA, 2019. (L)

Kalyn has always been an outcast in her small town, known as the kid whose dad committed murder when he was a teenager. She tries using a pseudonym at school, though it doesn't help much. One day she meets Gus, a kid who is tired of being known by either his disability, cerebral palsy, or the fact that his dad was murdered. Can they move past their history and generational trauma, or will the truth get in the way of friendship?

Awards and Honors
- Starred review: *Booklist*
- Anthony Award, Best Young Adult nominee, 2020
- Edgar Award, Best Young Adult nominee, 2020

Conversation Starters
1. Have you ever lived in a really small community? What was it like?
2. Is it difficult to be known for something you can't control—family, disability, circumstance, or something else?

You Don't Live Here by Robyn Schneider. Katherine Tegen Books, 2020. (B)

After losing her mother in an earthquake, Sasha is stuck moving in with her grandparents. They think they know what is best for her and all the things she needs to do to be perfect, but losing weight and dating the right boy are nowhere near Sasha's agenda. What is, though? A girl named Lily, who is ready to help Sasha off the road her grandparents seem set on making her travel.

Conversation Starters
1. What are some reasonable and unreasonable expectations for Sasha?
2. What path do you think Sasha should take?

SCIENCE FICTION

Alien: Echo by Mira Grant. Imprint, 2019. (L)

Set in the universe of the *Alien* movies, Olivia and her chronically ill twin sister, Viola, live on the planet Zagreus with their xenobiologist parents. When Olivia hosts a party for her sort-of girlfriend, Kora, and a few class-mates, deadly xenomorphs invade the planet—which also leads to the exposure of a shocking family secret. Olivia, Viola, and Kora must figure out a way to escape these terrifying aliens as well as adapt to how their lives have been turned completely upside down.

Conversation Starters
1. What do you think happened after they got on the ship at the end?
2. Were you expecting the reveal about Viola?

The Kindred by Alechia Dow. Inkyard Press, 2022. (A, B, P)

Joy was joined at birth to Duke Felix, and their minds are always connected, despite being so different. Joy is poor and marginalized, and Felix is rich, noble, and privileged. When the royal family is assassinated and Felix is blamed, he steals a ship to rescue Joy before anything can happen to her, and they crash-land on Earth.

Conversation Starters
1. How do themes of class play out in this book?
2. Do you believe it possible to find true love in such a setting?

The Sound of Stars by Alechia Dow. Inkyard Press, 2020. (A)

Two years after aliens invaded and one-third of humans were killed, Ellie lives in New York and runs a secret library of books and music, a secret that could get her killed. One of the aliens, M0Rr1S, finds the library, but instead of bringing in Ellie for execution, the two find common ground in art and go on the run.

Conversation Starters
1. What books, movies, songs, or art would you risk dying for?
2. Why do you believe the alien saved Ellie from execution?

SPECULATIVE FICTION

Pet by Akwaeke Emezi. Make Me a World, 2019. (T)
Bitter by Akwaeke Emezi. Knopf Books, 2022. (Q)

In *Pet,* Jam knows that monsters don't exist anymore, but when a creature with horns claws its way out of one of her mother's paintings and tells her it's a monster hunter, she's forced to confront the horrific truth living in her best friend Redemption's house.

Bitter is something of a prequel, following the title character caught between the mysterious school that gives her the chance to focus on her art and the reality of the protests against injustice in the streets of the town.

Awards and Honors
- Starred reviews, *Pet*: *Bulletin of the Center for Children's Books, Kirkus Reviews, Publishers Weekly, School Library Journal*
- Starred reviews, *Bitter*: *Kirkus Reviews, Publishers Weekly, School Library Journal*
- *Pet*: National Book Award for Young People's Literature finalist, 2019
- *Pet*: Otherwise Award nominee, 2019
- *Pet*: Carl Brandon Parallax Award, 2019
- *Pet*: Locus Award, Best Young Adult Book nominee, 2020
- *Pet*: Walter Dean Myers Award, Teen Category nominee, 2020
- *Pet*: Ignyte Award, Best Novel–YA nominee, 2020
- *Pet*: Rhode Island Teen Book Award nominee, 2021
- *Bitter*: Rainbow Book List, 2023

Conversation Starters
1. Does *Bitter* feel like a prequel to *Pet*? Why or why not?
2. What role does art play in *Pet* and *Bitter*? Is it the same in both books, or does it change?

ACTIVITIES, PROJECTS, AND PROGRAMS FOR YOUNGER TEENS

Duct Tape Pride Flags

If you have teens who like crafting with duct tape, it's fairly simple to make pride flags out of different colors of duct tape and either a pencil or a small dowel as a holder.

Pronoun Pins

Pronoun pins, like the one Harley wears in *The Heartbreak Bakery* (annotated in chapter 5), can be made using button makers, if available, or even cardboard or card stock, with a safety pin hot glued to the back and the front and sides protected with clear packing tape (see figure 4.2 for examples of pronoun pins). If you don't have a hot glue gun, you can use craft safety pins without the coil. Insert the safety pin from the back of your design, and then weave it in and out from one side of the design to the other.

FIGURE 4.2
Pronoun pins

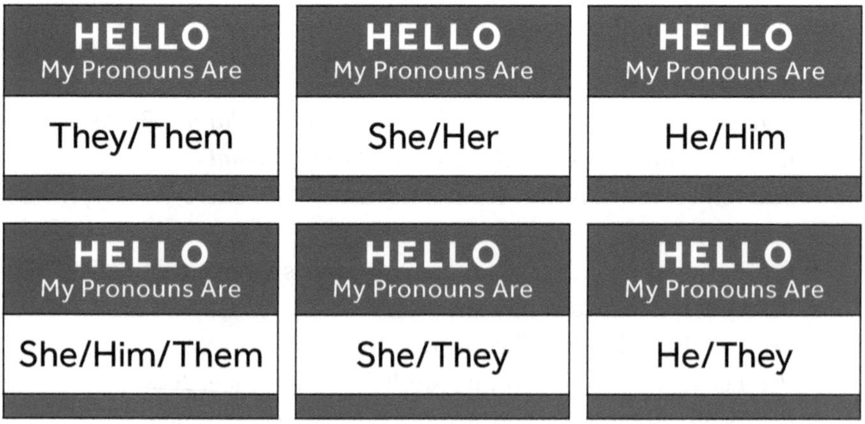

HELLO My Pronouns Are	**HELLO** My Pronouns Are	**HELLO** My Pronouns Are
They/Them	She/Her	He/Him
HELLO My Pronouns Are	**HELLO** My Pronouns Are	**HELLO** My Pronouns Are
She/Him/Them	She/They	He/They

'Zine-Making Programs

Some young people like to create blogs, Instagram posts, or other types of high-tech social media communication. Let's give young teens an opportunity to go old school by creating a 'zine. A *'zine* is defined as a self-published unique work of minority interest, usually reproduced via photocopier. Offer books like *Growing Up Trans, I Am Ace: Advice on Living Your Best Asexual Life*, or *The 57 Bus* as idea starters for topic 'zines. Young teens can select a topic or a group of people and research information for creation purposes. Copies could be made and shared with others.

WRAP-UP

Mental health is an important factor for all teens, but outside factors make mental health more of a challenge for LGBTQIA+ teens. Misgendering and deadnaming teens, like what happens to Felix in *Felix Ever After*, is incredibly harmful. Respecting names and pronouns, as with Syd and Harley in *The Heartbreak Bakery* (annotated in chapter 5), can significantly lower a trans or nonbinary teen's risk of self-harm or suicidality. If a student or patron confides in you that they're using a different name or pronoun set than you have in your records, especially if they tell you that it's not safe for them to do so at home or with family, respect the connection they've made with you, respect their identities, and, if at all possible, don't violate their trust.

NOTES

1. Laura Dattaro, "Largest Study to Date Confirms Overlap between Autism and Gender Diversity," *Spectrum, Autism Research News*, September 14, 2020, para. 1, www.spectrumnews.org/news/largest-study-to-date-confirms -overlap-between-autism-and-gender-diversity/.
2. Dattaro, "Study Confirms Overlap," para. 3.
3. The Trevor Project, *National Survey on LGBTQ Youth Mental Health 2021* (West Hollywood, CA: The Trevor Project, 2021), under "Introduction," www.thetrevorproject.org/survey-2021/.
4. The Trevor Project, *2022 National Survey on LGBTQ Youth Mental Health* (West Hollywood, CA: The Trevor Project, 2022), under "Impact of Current Events," www.thetrevorproject.org/survey-2022/.
5. Asperger's syndrome is now folded into the general autistic umbrella for a number of reasons.

Books and Conversation for Older Teens

A s teens move into young adulthood, they need more nuanced views of identities, relationships, and the problems and joys found in both, including discord, disappointment, and challenges, but also self-reliance, discovery, and opportunities. Reading books showing these issues and the way teens handle them gives them hope and encouragement that problems can be solved, issues can be confronted, and only sometimes does one live "happily ever after," but even temporary joy is better than none at all.

||||||||||||||||||||||

Voices from the Stacks
Shira Pilarski

A few older teens asked me for teen romance novels. As I often do, I went into the stacks with them, handing over an eclectic group of recommendations. After each teen had a small pile they were considering, one of the quieter ones came up to me. She whispered something, but I didn't quite get it. I asked her to repeat herself. In a slightly louder whisper, I heard, "Do you have any smut?" Her friends immediately started giggling uncontrollably, but I didn't hesitate. "Yes, we have plenty!" I handed over a few teen titles, and then I mentioned a few in the adult fiction section, letting them know that the adult titles would have more extensive and graphic sex scenes. I made sure to include a variety of queer titles, clearly stating the genders and orientations of the characters. The teens seemed particularly impressed and excited to read books about characters with different identities than theirs. I was struck by how important it is for young people to have a window, not only into the day-to-day lived experiences of people who are different from them, but into how sex plays into different people's lives. Teens are learning about different aspects of adulthood and deciding who they want to be as adults. It is imperative that they are allowed—and encouraged—to find their paths through the safe sexual exploration afforded to them in books.

||||||||||||||||||||||

Start Small
The First Older Teen Books to Add to Your Collection

- *Gender Queer: A Memoir* by Maia Kobabe
- *Mooncakes* by Suzanne Walker and Wendy Xu
- *Hell Followed with Us* by Andrew Joseph White

TRENDS IN OLDER TEEN LGBTQIA+ BOOKS

Books for older LGBTQIA+ teens often include fewer parental figures, as in *Hell Followed with Us* and *As Far As You'll Take Me*; more focus on relationships, such as in *Destination Unknown* and *Let's Talk about Love*; self-sufficiency, as in *Self-Made Boys* and *Loveless*; and plots that don't revolve around high school, such as in *Missing, Presumed Dead* and in *How to Excavate a Heart*.

SPECIAL FOCUS: HOMELESSNESS

Homelessness is an issue that disproportionately affects LGBTQIA+ youth, and books such as *Just Ash* (annotated in chapter 4), *Hell Followed with Us*, and *Surviving the City* all tackle different ways that teens can be homeless. In *Just Ash*, Ash runs away from home when his mother takes the start of Ash's period as a sign that instead of continuing to raise Ash as a boy, which they have been doing since he was born intersex, Ash should "try to be normal" and give living as a girl a chance. Benji runs away from a genocidal religious cult with his father in *Hell Followed with Us*; while his father supports Benji's transition, the rest of the cult does not, and that's not even remotely close to the worst parts of the cult. Dez is living in a group home in *Surviving the City, Vol. 2: From the Roots Up* after her grandmother dies from complications of diabetes; she's discovering that she is two spirit, and the home forbids relationships between residents, like that between her and her girlfriend, Kacey.

||||||||||||||||||||||

Voices from the Stacks
Kathleen Breitenbach

When I was growing up, my stepfather (or *wicked stepmother* as he sometimes termed himself) always took in strays. Sometimes that manifested in a student bringing him a kitten found in a convertible in the school's parking lot and him adopting it, and sometimes that manifested in taking people in. We used to joke that my dad was one of his strays. As an adult, I developed the same mindset, never wanting to turn away a stray cat or human. When one of my partner's friends was coming out to her family as trans, she worried they wouldn't take it well and she'd have no place to live. My stepfather was deep in my heart at that moment, and we promised that she'd always have a place with us. Eventually she was able to move on, get her own place, and be independent, but I know it would have been much harder if she'd been living out of her car, couch surfing, or on the street. Despite being in the twenty-first century and living in a fairly progressive state, parents kicking their kids out for being LGBTQIA+ still happens.

According to True Colors United, "4.2 million youth experience homelessness each year."[1] The findings are worse for LGBTQIA+ youth; the Voices of Youth Count study through the University of Chicago found that LGBTQIA+

> youth had a 120% increased risk of experiencing homelessness compared to youth who identified as heterosexual and cisgender. These findings reinforce growing evidence on the heightened risk of experiencing homelessness among LGBT youth. This often stems from a

lack of acceptance that young people experience both in and outside of the home.[2]

The Trevor Project makes clear that these findings reflect an even more desperate situation:

> 28% of LGBTQ youth reported experiencing homelessness or housing instability at some point in their lives—and those who did had two to four times the odds of reporting depression, anxiety, self-harm, considering suicide, and attempting suicide compared to those with stable housing.[3]

And this isn't a new issue. Sylvia Rivera and Marsha P. Johnson founded STAR, Street Transvestite Action Revolutionaries, specifically to help and house the many homeless LGBT youth in Lower Manhattan in 1970, as many queer youth were either runaways or throwaways.[4]

Trauma-informed services are important for any teacher or librarian, but they are essential when serving LGBTQIA+ youth (and adults). For LGBTQIA+ homeless teens, it may not be safe for runaways to go back home. Not all shelters will accept LGBTQIA+ teens, and some might inflict more trauma on the very teens who need help. If your school or library has a food pantry for homeless students or patrons, make sure that your LGBTQIA+ teens also know about it. Frequently teens will couch surf and stay with friends, bouncing from house to house, so they may not seem at a glance to be experiencing housing insecurity, and many people who are homeless don't necessarily look like the stereotypical picture of someone who is dirty and smelly, with torn clothing.

OLDER TEEN BOOKS THAT CAN BE USED IN OTHER DISPLAYS

Black History Month

Ace of Spades

All Boys Aren't Blue: A Memoir
  Manifesto

Darling

Let's Talk about Love

This Poison Heart

This Wicked Fate

We Are Not Broken

You Should See Me in a Crown

Hispanic Heritage Month

Blanca and Roja

Burn Down, Rise Up

Cemetery Boys

The Hazards of Love, Book 1:
  Bright World

The Mirror Season

Ophelia After All

Self-Made Boys: A Great Gatsby
  Remix

They Both Die at the End

We Set the Dark on Fire

We Unleash the Merciless Storm

Asian American and Pacific Islander Month

Cold

How It All Blew Up

The Loophole

The Love and Lies of Rukhsana Ali

Mooncakes

Picture Us in the Light

The Red Scrolls of Magic

St. Patrick's Day/Irish

All the Bad Apples

Ironspark

Summer

Indestructible Object

Winter Holidays

How to Excavate a Heart

Native American Heritage Month

Surviving the City, Vol. 2: From the Roots Up

FANTASY

The Afterward by E. K. Johnston. Dutton Books/Penguin, 2019. (B, L, Q)

Set in the year after an epic quest, two heroes are thrust apart when Apprentice Knight Kalanthe must find a way to pay off her Knight School loans and it looks like the only option is to find a husband, and thief Olsa discovers that the notoriety from the quest makes it hard for her to blend in and ply her trade.

Awards and Honors
- Starred review: *School Library Journal*

Conversation Starters
1. What impact does this book have by turning typical fantasy tropes of male-dominated societies and knighthoods into a queer-normative society with women in more equal roles?
2. Was there enough world building, or did it feel more like fanfiction instead of fantasy?

Belle Révolte by Linsey Miller. Sourcebooks Fire, 2020. (A, L)

Emilie would much rather be a physician than go to finishing school, learning embroidery and divination, and Annette longs to escape her family and learn magic. During a chance meeting, the girls switch lives. But when war and truth break out, their rebellions become bigger than just two people.

Conversation Starters
1. How can personal desires outweigh what's good for the larger community?
2. Have you ever wanted to trade places with someone totally different from you?

Beyond the Ruby Veil by Mara Fitzgerald. Little, Brown Books for Young Readers, 2020. (L, G)

Emanuela's world is one in which water is incredibly scarce; the only source is a creature that uses magic to turn blood into water from those unlucky enough to develop an omen on their skin. When Emanuela's omen is discovered during her wedding despite years of hiding it, she's taken away and, in the struggle, accidentally kills the *watercrea*. Before everyone dies of dehydration, she has to try to figure out how to get water back, and that means going through the veil to find the source of the *watercrea*'s power.

Awards and Honors
- Starred review: *School Library Journal*

Conversation Starters
1. How would you compare this story to today's world and the issue of water scarcity?
2. What do you think of the premise of this story—killing people for water?

Black Wings Beating by Alex London. Farrar, Straus and Giroux Books for Young Readers, 2018. (A, G)

Red Skies Falling by Alex London. Farrar, Straus and Giroux Books for Young Readers, 2019. (A, G)

Gold Wings Rising by Alex London. Farrar, Straus and Giroux Books for Young Readers, 2020. (A, G, T, Q)

Brysen and Kylee live in a world centered around birds and the sky, and while Brysen wants to be a falconer, Kylee wants nothing to do with falconry. Unfortunately, war is brewing, and the only thing that might save the Six Villages is finding and using a mythic ghost eagle.

Awards and Honors
- Starred reviews, *Black Wings Beating*: *Kirkus Reviews*, *School Library Journal*
- Starred review, *Red Skies Falling*: *Kirkus Reviews*

Conversation Starters

1. How is Brysen and Kylee's world impacted by society revolving around birds and the sky?
2. Have you ever had an interest in falconry? How about the study of birds?

The Brilliant Death by A. R. Capetta. Viking Books for Young Readers, 2018. (Q)

Teo is a strega who has just turned one of her father's enemies into a music box when a stray cloud materializes into a person on the mountain. After her father is poisoned and the heads of the other Five Families murdered, Teo and Cielo use their strega powers to confront the person responsible in Vinalia's capital.

Awards and Honors

- Starred reviews: *Kirkus Reviews, School Library Journal*

Conversation Starters

1. If you had magic to change any part of your appearance, would you, and if so, what would you change?
2. What role does sexism play in this story?

Carry On by Rainbow Rowell. St. Martin's Press, 2015. (Q)

Wayward Son by Rainbow Rowell. Wednesday Books, 2019. (Q)

Any Way the Wind Blows by Rainbow Rowell. Wednesday Books, 2021. (Q)

After defeating the Mage and the Insidious Humdrum in *Carry On*, Simon, his boyfriend Baz, and their friend Penny should be getting along fine, but without magic, Simon is a moody couch potato with wings, and Baz has had about enough. When they get the chance to travel to the United States, it seems like the perfect opportunity for a change of pace, and to get Simon out of his funk.

Simon, Baz, and their friends had their world turned upside-down in *Carry On* and *Wayward Son*. Back in England for *Any Way the Wind Blows,* the friends have to figure out what kind of lives they want to live, or even if they want to stay connected to the World of Mages at all.

Awards and Honors
- Starred review, *Wayward Son: Booklist*
- Starred review, *Any Way the Wind Blows: Booklist*
- *Wayward Son*: Goodreads Choice Award, Young Adult Fantasy and Science Fiction nominee, 2019
- *Wayward Son*: Teens' Top Ten, 2020
- *Any Way the Wind Blows*: Goodreads Choice Award, Young Adult Fantasy and Science Fiction nominee, 2021

Conversation Starters
1. There's a lot of trauma for the characters to process. In what way does the road trip affect each character?
2. Was it interesting to get a story about what happens after a Chosen One finishes what they are supposed to do?

Ironspark by C. M. McGuire. Swoon Reads, 2020. (B, P, Q, A)

Bryn's mother was abducted by the Fae, and to try to get her back, Bryn learns all she can with the help of two classmates and a water witch.

Conversation Starters
1. How do the Fae in *Ironspark* differ from how you typically think of fairies?
2. How are themes of mental illness treated in this book?

The Red Scrolls of Magic by Cassandra Clare and Wesley Chu. Margaret K. McElderry Books, 2019. (G, B)

Part of the Shadowhunters universe and the first book in the Eldest Curses series, *The Red Scrolls of Magic* features High Warlock Magnus Bane and his new boyfriend, Alec Lightwood. Readers don't need knowledge of previous books in this universe to enjoy the wild ride as Bane, Lightwood, and a cast of diverse characters tear through Europe on a quest to stop a demon-worshiping cult so they can go back to enjoying their vacation together.

Awards and Honors
- Goodreads Choice Award, Fantasy nominee, 2019

Conversation Starters
1. If one or more participants in a relationship is immortal, what is the dividing line between acceptable and unacceptable age differences?
2. If you were traveling around with someone who could make portals to anywhere, where would you want to go?

***Ship of Smoke and Steel* by Django Wexler. Tor Teen, 2019. (B)**

***City of Stone and Silence* by Django Wexler. Tor Teen, 2020. (B, Q)**

***Siege of Rage and Ruin* by Django Wexler. Tor Teen, 2021. (B, Q)**

Isoka uses combat magic to survive and keep her younger sister safe. But when she's captured and blackmailed into stealing a legendary ghost ship, she finds herself in a battle with the rest of the crew, the creatures on the ship, and her feelings for a fellow crewmember and princess.

In book 2, Isoka continues trying to gain control of the ghost ship, but it's docked itself on an island with more danger and horror around every corner, and Tori proves she's not the sheltered innocent that Isoka believes her to be.

In book 3, Isoka has finally captured the ship, *Soliton*, and returns to free her sister, Tori, only to find that Tori has somehow started a rebellion.

Conversation Starters
1. Does a protagonist have to be likable to be interesting?
2. Does Isoka's upbringing excuse her choices?

We Set the Dark on Fire by Tehlor Kay Mejia. Katherine Tegen Books, 2019. (L)

We Unleash the Merciless Storm by Tehlor Kay Mejia. Katherine Tegan Books, 2020. (L)

Daniela Vargas is the top student at the Medio School for Girls, and she's sure to be picked as one of two wives of one of the most influential young men in the town. Nothing in school has prepared her for the reality of the family she marries into, much less what happens when she's asked to spy for the resistance or to fall in love with someone else.

The sequel to *We Set the Dark on Fire* follows Carmen this time, whose undercover identity as part of the resistance group has been exposed. The island is staring down the start of a civil war, and La Voz somehow doesn't seem to be the same group it used to be.

Awards and Honors

- Starred reviews, *We Set the Dark on Fire*: *Booklist, Kirkus Reviews, Publishers Weekly, School Library Journal*
- Starred reviews, *We Unleash the Merciless Storm*: *Booklist, Kirkus Reviews*
- *We Set the Dark on Fire*: Rise: A Feminist Book Project List, 2020

Conversation Starters

1. Daniela and Carmen's relationship could be considered an example of the enemies-to-lovers trope in storytelling. Does that aspect of their unfolding relationship have any parallels to Daniela's involvement with the La Voz?
2. How does Daniela's life speak to the current treatment of immigrants and refugees?
3. Community is especially important in this book. In what communities does Carmen find herself, and how do they impact her choices?
4. In what ways do class differences drive the narrative?

The Witch King by H. E. Edgmon. Inkyard Press, 2021. (T, G, A, P, Q)

The Fae Keeper by H. E. Edgmon. Inkyard Press, 2022. (T, G, A, P, Q)

When Wyatt was young, he was betrothed to a fae prince, despite the fact that Wyatt is a witch and the fae don't particularly hold witches in any kind of regard. After his magic got out of control one night and his parents died, Wyatt ran. But now Prince Emyr has to bring Wyatt back to the kingdom, or else.

Awards and Honors
- Starred review, *The Witch King*: *Publishers Weekly*

Conversation Starters
1. How is family shown in this duology?
2. In the second book in the Witch King series, the Prince and the Fae are together, but their kingdom is in danger of failing. Should the prince choose love or country?

GRAPHIC NONFICTION

Gender Queer: A Memoir by Maia Kobabe. Oni Press, 2019. (T, Nonbinary, A)

Maia Kobabe's *Gender Queer* is a memoir charting the growth and discovery of the author through eir journey to figuring out that e is nonbinary. With beautiful illustrations and painfully vulnerable confessions, *Gender Queer* is a love letter to queer teens, telling them that they are not alone in having thoughts and feelings that they may assume are unique to them.

Awards and Honors
- Starred review: *School Library Journal*
- Stonewall Honor Book in Non-Fiction, 2020
- Alex Award, 2020

Conversation Starters
1. There are a lot of challenges of this book in schools, in libraries, and in specific states. Why do you think it has gotten such a strong reaction?

2. Throughout the book, Maia shows how much e had to learn from books, libraries, and fandoms instead of learning about them in school. What do you think schools should be teaching but aren't?
3. Has working on creating something for a fandom helped you be more creative in original works?

Welcome to St. Hell: My Trans Teen Misadventure by Lewis Hancox. Scholastic Graphix, 2022. (T)

Lewis narrates the story of his teen years, showing how difficult it can be to experience gender dysphoria, especially when a teen hasn't figured out yet that what they're experiencing is gender dysphoria.

Awards and Honors
• Rainbow Book List, 2023

Conversation Starters
1. Although this story takes place in the United Kingdom, is it similar to what happens in the United States?
2. Do you think the graphic novel format was the best choice for this book? Why or why not?

GRAPHIC NOVELS

The Hazards of Love, Book 1: Bright World by Stan Stanley. Oni Press, 2021. (T, Nonbinary)

Amparo wants to be a better person, or at least to be thought of better than they are, so that Iolanthe might be willing to date them. Unfortunately for Amparo, the deal that they make with the talking cat that shows up at their window one night has unseen repercussions, and while the cat is walking around in Amparo's body, Amparo is stuck in a spirit world, trying to find a way to escape.

Awards and Honors
• Starred reviews: *Booklist, Kirkus Reviews, School Library Journal*
• Great Graphic Novels for Teens Top Ten, 2022

Conversation Starters
1. What would be tempting enough for you to make a deal with a strange and supernatural creature?
2. How did you feel about Amparo's adventures in the spirit world?

Lifetime Passes by Terry Blas. Abrams ComicArts–Surely, 2021. (Q)

Jackie's parents have been deported, and she lives with her Tía Gina. When Gina announces that they can no longer afford to buy season passes to the amusement park that she loves so dearly, Jackie has an idea. Tía Gina works at an assisted living facility for the elderly, and there's a secret rule that Jackie has discovered: "If a member of their party dies at the park, the rest of their group gets free lifetime passes." She and her friends decide to "volunteer" to take residents to the park, secretly hoping one of the seniors will pass away. They quickly realize, though, that some of the residents have even closer ties to the park than they thought.

Conversation Starters
1. Does age matter in a friendship?
2. Have you ever done something good for a selfish motive?

Mooncakes by Suzanne Walker and Wendy Xu. Oni Press, 2019. (Nonbinary, Q)

Nova works with her grandmothers in their bookshop, pouring over spell-books and tracking anything supernatural, when one day she hears about a wolf. When she investigates, the wolf turns out to be her friend and child-hood crush, Tam, who's now a werewolf. Now back in each other's lives, will sparks fly?

Awards and Honors
- Starred review: *School Library Journal*
- Goodreads Choice Award, Graphic Novels and Comics nominee, 2019
- Cybils Award finalist, 2019
- Novels and Comics nominee, 2019
- Rainbow Book List Top Ten, 2020

- Hugo Award for Best Graphic Story or Comic nominee, 2020
- Rhode Island Teen Book Award nominee, 2022

Conversation Starters

1. Magic spellbooks, childhood crushes—what more would you add to this story?
2. Is there anything you would add to this story to make it more convincing?

Surviving the City, Vol. 2: From the Roots Up by Tasha Spillett, illustrated by Natasha Donovan. Highwater Press, 2020. (2S)

After Dez's grandmother passes away, Dez ends up in a group home and meets Kacey. When Dez, Kacey, Dez's best friend Miikwan, and new kid Riel attend an afterschool program for Indigenous students, Riel helps show everyone how to be more inclusive of two spirit relatives like Dez.

Awards and Honors

- Indigenous Voices Award for Published Graphic Novels, Comics, and Illustrated Books in Any Language nominee, 2021

Conversation Starters

1. Do you know what the term *two spirit* (2S) means?
2. How do you support your friends who are in an underserved population?

Taproot by Keezy Young. Oni Press, 2017. (G)

Hamal is one of the few people who can see Blue, because Blue's a ghost. When something strange starts happening to the other ghosts in town, Hamal begins to investigate. And then a Reaper shows up and tells them that florist Hamal is, accidentally, a necromancer.

Conversation Starters

1. What insights to the story can you discover by looking at the color palette?
2. Could a relationship between a live human and a ghost work?

HISTORICAL FICTION

Destination Unknown by Bill Konigsberg. Scholastic Press, 2022. (G)

When Micah first spots C. J. on the dance floor, he is both enthralled and intimidated by someone who is so obviously not hiding his queer identity, while Micah lives with his protective and slightly conservative Jewish parents. Amid the backdrop of 1987 New York City, with music and the AIDS epidemic pounding, there's a fine line between being independent and being on your own.

Awards and Honors
- Starred reviews: *Booklist, Kirkus Reviews*

Conversation Starters
1. C. J. helps his community by volunteering with God's Love We Deliver. In what ways do you serve your community?
2. What is the first album you would recommend to someone that would encapsulate who you are?

Self-Made Boys: A Great Gatsby Remix by Anna-Marie McLemore. Feiwel and Friends, 2022. (T, G, L)

Nick is moving from his small town in Minnesota to rent a cottage from his cousin Daisy just outside of New York City. While Nick is busy trying to pass as a normal (i.e., not transgender) guy, Daisy's busy doing everything she can to pass as white and not Latinx. Things get more complicated when Nick gets drawn into the life of his neighbor, Jay, who throws extravagant parties at his mansion and has secrets of his own.

Awards and Honors
- Starred reviews: *Booklist, Kirkus Reviews*

Conversation Starters
1. If you've read *The Great Gatsby,* how does this retelling change things?
2. A lot of books feature a token gay or queer character. Does this book seem like it has a token straight character?

HORROR

Burn Down, Rise Up by Vincent Tirado. Sourcebooks Fire, 2022. (L)

Racquel's been trying not to think about how many teens have been going missing in the Bronx. The police pay attention only when it's the white kids who are gone. But when her crush's cousin goes missing one night and her mom's fallen sick with something nobody can identify, she has to do something. Racquel and Charlize team up to figure out what's going on, what the Echo Game is, and what happened to the Bronx decades before.

Awards and Honors
- Pura Belpré Young Adult Author Award, 2023

Conversation Starters
1. Are there any urban legends from where you've grown up?
2. Do you know the real history of your town? Is it different from what was taught in school?

Hell Followed with Us by Andrew Joseph White. Peachtree Teen, 2022. (T, G, Q)

Benji's trying to get away from the genocidal religious cult that's already released a virus that killed most of the world's population and is now working on one that will turn someone into a horrifyingly biblically accurate angel-monster. His father is killed in the escape, but luckily Benji finds a group of teen survivors in town who are using the local LGBTQ center as a home and base of operations.

Awards and Honors
- Starred reviews: *Booklist, Kirkus Reviews, Publishers Weekly*
- William C. Morris Award finalist, 2023
- Rainbow Book List, 2023

Conversation Starters
1. How does this book deal with issues of body horror, both in terms of gender dysphoria and in terms of characters turning into literal monsters?
2. What element of this story caused you to read it?

MAGICAL REALISM ─────────────────────────────

||||||||||||||||||||||||

Authors You Should Know
Anna-Marie McLemore

Anna-Marie McLemore writes lyrical novels full of magical realism, the exception being *Self-Made Boys: A Great Gatsby Remix*, which is not magical realism, but the prose is possibly even more well written than their previous works. Their works usually contain at least one transgender or nonbinary character, and themes of family—particularly found family, acceptance, love, and overcoming obstacles—are prevalent. *Dark and Deepest Red* is a work that focuses on the dancing plague of 1518 in Strasbourg, anchoring its themes of otherness and acceptance in the very real mania that encompassed the town. Most of their other work centers around Latinx/Latine characters, and newer works like *Lakelore* also include characters who have ADHD and are dyslexic. The intersectional aspects of race, disability, and neurodiversity, combined with folklore and current issues, make McLemore's books especially valuable in connecting many different groups of teens. *The Mirror Season* could be used in a discussion about consent, *Self-Made Boys* could be used in a compare-and-contrast with F. Scott Fitzgerald's *The Great Gatsby,* and many of the books could also be used when discussing historical fiction.

Blanca and Roja by Anna-Marie McLemore. Macmillan/Feiwel and Friends, 2018. (T)

Legend says that there are always two daughters in the del Cisne family, and after the younger sister turns fifteen, one of the two will change into a swan. When two missing kids suddenly reappear in the woods, the sisters' lives get even more complicated.

Awards and Honors
- Starred reviews: *Booklist, Kirkus Reviews, School Library Journal*

Conversation Starters

1. *Blanca and Roja* contains some of the same themes as folk tales surrounding Snow White and Rose Red and the Swan Maiden and Swan Lake. In what ways does this retelling speak to modern themes and social issues?
2. In what ways does McLemore explore Page's experiences with gender and gender identity?

Cemetery Boys by Aiden Thomas. Swoon Reads, 2020. (T, G)

Since Yadriel's family doesn't seem to have accepted his transition in more than name, he intends to prove that he is a real brujo by summoning his cousin Miguel in a sacred ritual. He accidentally summons Julian—an attractive, sarcastic bad boy—instead. Now he must find a way to convince Julian to let him set his spirit free, complete the ritual, and also figure out what really happened to Miguel. Unfortunately, the more time Yadriel spends with Julian, the less he wants to let him go, and the more Julian seems to want to stick around too.

Awards and Honors

- Starred reviews: *Booklist, Publishers Weekly*
- Bram Stoker Award for Best Young Adult Novel nominee, 2020
- Goodreads Choice Award, Young Adult Fantasy and Science Fiction nominee and Debut Novel nominee, 2020
- Lodestar Award nominee, 2021
- Locus Award for Best First Novel nominee, 2021
- Rhode Island Teen Book Award nominee, 2022

Conversation Starters

1. How does Yadriel feel about his family's unwillingness to accept his new pronouns? How do you know?
2. Family is very important to the characters in this story, though some of the families look different from others. What do you think defines a family? How do the families in the story affect the main characters?

Dark and Deepest Red by Anna-Marie McLemore. Feiwel and Friends, 2020. (T)

A dancing plague consumed the residents of Strasbourg in 1518, and Lala is sure that she and her aunt will be blamed since they are Romani. In the present day, Lala's descendent is determined to find out what really happened, especially since her friend has put on her own family's famous red shoes and now can't stop dancing either.

Awards and Honors
- Starred reviews: *Booklist, Kirkus Reviews*

Conversation Starters
1. Had you ever heard of the dancing plague before?
2. The modern-day portion is a retelling of "The Red Shoes" folktale. How well does that fit in with the historical events?

The Gentleman's Guide to Vice and Virtue by Mackenzi Lee. Katherine Tegen Books, 2017. (B)

The Lady's Guide to Petticoats and Piracy by Mackenzi Lee. Katherine Tegen Books, 2018. (A, B)

Henry Montague, known as Monty, is a rake and a rogue. Determined to spite his father, he spends his days and nights drinking and cavorting with all types of people. But as a member of the aristocracy, he's expected to go on a grand tour of Europe before settling down and learning how to behave. His best friend and secret crush, Percy, accompanies him, and his sister Felicity is being shipped off to learn to be more ladylike. Monty knows that he has only this one trip to make Percy fall in love with him, but his decision-making skills leave much to be desired, and they fall into several harrowing situations. Everyone has secrets, and before this tour is over, those secrets will find a way of coming out.

Felicity Montague got plenty of adventure with her brother Henry and his best friend/boyfriend Percy in *The Gentleman's Guide to Vice and Virtue*. Now, after getting stuck in Scotland working in a bakery because no medical school will admit her as a student, Felicity sets off to try to find somewhere that will. Along the way, she becomes embroiled in intrigue with her childhood best friend and more adventures across Europe.

Awards and Honors
- Starred reviews, *The Gentleman's Guide to Vice and Virtue*: *Booklist, Kirkus Reviews, Publishers Weekly, School Library Journal*
- Starred reviews, *The Lady's Guide to Petticoats and Piracy*: *Booklist, Kirkus Reviews, School Library Journal*
- *The Gentleman's Guide to Vice and Virtue*: Goodreads Choice Award, Young Adult Fiction nominee, 2017
- *The Gentleman's Guide to Vice and Virtue*: Stonewall Honor Book in Children's Literature, 2018
- *The Lady's Guide to Petticoats and Piracy*: Goodreads Choice Award, Young Adult Fiction nominee, 2018
- *The Gentleman's Guide to Vice and Virtue*: Rhode Island Teen Book Award nominee, 2019
- *The Lady's Guide to Petticoats and Piracy*: Amelia Bloomer Book List, 2019

Conversation Starters
1. Where would you go if you went on a tour of Europe?
2. Have you ever had a crush on a friend?
3. How much, if anything, do you know about asexuality?
4. How cool are dragons?

The Heartbreak Bakery by A. R. Capetta. Candlewick Press, 2021. (T, Q, Nonbinary)

Syd is working in a queer bakery in Austin and has just been dumped. There must be some extra ingredients when everyone who eats Syd's breakup brownies also breaks up. Syd has to find some way to stop this chain reaction, especially since the couple who owns the bakery get caught up in the unfortunate brownies. Luckily the store's delivery person, Harley, believes Syd, and the two vow to fix the problems Syd's brownies have caused.

Awards and Honors
- Starred review: *Booklist*
- Lambda Literary Award for LGBTQ Young Adult, 2022
- Best Fiction for Young Adults, 2022

Conversation Starters
1. Syd is an agender cupcake. If you were a gender or sexuality mixed with a baked good, what would you be?
2. Who is your favorite character in this book?

Lakelore by Anna-Marie McLemore. Feiwel and Friends, 2022. (T, L, Nonbinary)

Bastián and Lore have both seen the world under the water, though it's been years since they've spoken. To the rest of the town, it's just rumor or urban legend, until the worlds start merging. Bastián and Lore are forced to team up to stop it, especially if they don't want the secrets they're keeping under the water to rise up.

Awards and Honors
- Starred reviews: *Booklist, Kirkus Reviews, Publishers Weekly*
- Rainbow Book List, 2023

Conversation Starters
1. What metaphors can you see in the underwater world? Does it serve as a visible representation of queerness, transness, and/or neurodiversity?
2. Do the alternating points of view add to this story? Why or why not?

The Loophole by Naz Kutub. Bloomsbury, 2022. (G)

Syeed is moping because his boyfriend Farouk left, and while Sy was invited along, he declined, and all he can do now is wish for another chance. So when a girl literally collides with the front of the coffee shop where Sy works and offers him three wishes, who could say no?

Awards and Honors
- Rainbow Book List, 2023

Conversation Starters
1. Do you think Reggie is really a Djinn or just rich?
2. Is money its own kind of magic?

The Lost Coast by A. R. Capetta. Candlewick Press, 2019. (Q)

Danny is drawn to the wild California redwood coast by a coven of queer teen witches called the Grays. They are convinced that Danny is the only one who can save their leader, Imogen, who has disappeared—and who also may be either a victim or the cause of some deadly magic that has settled there.

Awards and Honors
- Starred review: *Booklist*

Conversation Starters
1. How much impact does the setting have on the plot?
2. Did you relate to any of the Grays? If so, which one(s), and if not, why not?

The Mirror Season by Anna-Marie McLemore. Feiwel and Friends, 2021. (P)

Graciela and Lock were both sexually assaulted at a party, though their memories of it vary. Afterward, Ciela loses the ability to make magical pan dulce, trees are vanishing, and objects are turning into sharp mirrors before Ciela's eyes. Ciela might be able to help Lock, but helping and telling the truth could be two very different things.

Awards and Honors
- Starred reviews: *Booklist, Kirkus Reviews, Publishers Weekly, School Library Journal*
- National Book Award for Young People's Literature nominee, 2021
- Best Fiction for Young Adults, 2022

Conversation Starters
1. Can two people with different memories of an event both be right? Discuss an example you know about.
2. What does it take to overcome a trauma? How do people use different methods of coping?

This Poison Heart by Kalynn Bayron. Bloomsbury YA, 2021. (L)

This Wicked Fate by Kalynn Bayron. Bloomsbury, 2022. (L)

Briseis has a special gift that allows her to grow plants with a single touch and an immunity to poison plants that would otherwise cause intense pain and death. Life has not been easy for Briseis, her two moms, and their flower shop that may have to close due to an upcoming spike in the rent. Everything changes when Briseis receives word that she is the last living heir to her birth family's estate located in the small town of Rhinebeck. Surrounded by an enormous amount of land and plants, Briseis will finally be able to let loose and see what she can do with her gift. She finds that she has inherited more than just a sprawling estate—a house full of secrets, a poison garden, and an apothecary that the locals rely on—but not everyone is happy to have her in town.

In *This Wicked Fate*, Briseis, one of her moms, and her new friends set off to find the other pieces of the heart to try to bring her other mom back from the dead.

Awards and Honors
- Starred reviews, *This Poison Heart*: *Booklist, Publishers Weekly*
- *This Poison Heart*: Best Fiction for Young Adults, 2022
- *This Poison Heart*: Rainbow Book List Top Ten for Teen Readers, 2022

Conversation Starters
1. Where do you think Briseis's gift comes from?
2. Do you think there are others who have the same gift?
3. Why is Briseis able to handle poisons that others cannot?
4. If you could have any special ability, what would you choose and why?

MYSTERY

All the Things We Do in the Dark by Saundra Mitchell. HarperCollins/ HarperTeen, 2019. (Q)

Something happened when Ava was nine; the scar on her face is proof of that much. After spending years trying to build a life and stuff trauma down, she trips over a dead body in the woods while walking back from getting a tattoo. Is this death and her trauma connected in any way other than in Ava's mind? And what about Haley, the cute girl Ava's falling for, who happens to be the daughter of the first in a string of police officers she talked to all those years ago?

Awards and Honors
- Starred review: *Bulletin of the Center for Children's Books*
- Lambda Literary Award for Children and Young Adults finalist, 2019

Conversation Starters
1. Ava's story is about survivorship and the choices we make because of and in spite of trauma. Why does Ava make the choice to investigate Jane's death on her own instead of contacting the police?
2. Does Ava's relationship with Haley help her heal?

Cold by Mariko Tamaki. Roaring Brook Press, 2022. (G, L)

Told in dual point of view, *Cold* relates the story of two teens, Todd, whose body was found in the snow, and Georgia, who's trying to solve his murder. Nobody at Todd's school wants to talk about him or what might have happened to him, and Georgia can't shake the feeling that she's seen this boy before.

Conversation Starters
1. What do you do when you pass by someone you think you know?
2. How do the two points of view help the story flow?

Darling by K. Ancrum. Imprint, 2021. (A, B, L, Q)

On Wendy Darling's first night in Chicago, a boy shows up in her window, saying his name is Peter and inviting her out with his friends. Soon she's involved with Tinkerbelle and the Lost Boys and on the run from Chicago PD Detective Hook. Slowly, Wendy learns that not everything about Peter and his friends is as it appears, and she may be in danger from more than just Hook.

Conversation Starters
1. How would you compare this book to the original Peter Pan story?
2. What other Peter Pan variations have you read?

Even If We Break by Marieke Nijkamp. Sourcebooks Fire, 2020. (T, Nonbinary, B)

It was supposed to be one last gaming weekend for a group of friends invested in a live-action role-playing game; but the fun, cozy cabin for five friends turns sinister quickly, and soon the friends are forced to figure out what's in the game and what's real.

Conversation Starters

1. Have you ever been to an escape room?
2. What would you do if you were stuck in a live-action role-playing game and lives were on the line?

Missing, Presumed Dead by Emma Berquist. Greenwillow Books, 2019. (L)

When Lexi touches someone, she sees the exact moment that person will die. Not only that, she can also see ghosts. It's a lot to handle, and she frequently takes breaks in a psychiatric ward just so that she doesn't accidentally get touched. One night, she literally bumps into a girl who Lexi knows will be murdered mere hours later. Can Lexi and Jane's ghost solve the murder and stop the perpetrators before they kill again?

Conversation Starters

1. What would you do if you could see and talk to ghosts?
2. Is Lexi's plan of checking herself in and out of psychiatric hospitals sustainable?

NONFICTION

All Boys Aren't Blue: A Memoir-Manifesto by George M. Johnson. Farrar, Straus and Giroux, 2020. (Q, G, T)

We Are Not Broken by George M. Johnson. Little, Brown Books for Young Readers, 2021. (Nonbinary, Q)

George M. Johnson tells stories from their youth growing up in New Jersey and examines the Black and queer context. Though their family was loving and supportive, they faced pervasive homophobia, queerphobia, and racism.

We Are Not Broken continues the narrative from *All Boys Aren't Blue* and goes into more depth about Johnson's Nanny, who had just passed away.

Awards and Honors
- Starred review, *All Boys Aren't Blue*: *Kirkus Reviews*
- Starred review, *We Are Not Broken*: *Booklist*
- *All Boys Aren't Blue*: Goodreads Choice Award, Memoir and Autobiography nominee, 2020
- *All Boys Aren't Blue*: Teens' Top Ten, 2021

Conversation Starters
1. George endures a lot of traumas growing up. What was the hardest to read about?
2. Would George's story be significantly different if they weren't both Black and queer, just one or the other?

REALISTIC FICTION

Ace of Spades by Faridah Àbíké-Íyímídé. Feiwel & Friends, 2021. (G)

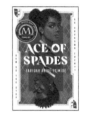

Devon Richards and Chiamaka Adebayo couldn't have more different experiences at the prestigious Niveus Private School. Devon is a quiet music student on scholarship working on his audition piece for Julliard, while Chiamaka is the most popular girl in school, doing all she can to secure her admittance to Yale. What they do have in common is that they have both been chosen to be Senior Prefects, and they happen to be the only two African American students at the school. Not long after their appointment, a mysterious enemy, known only as Aces, starts to send anonymous texts that reveal many of Devon's and Chiamaka's darkest secrets.

Awards and Honors
- Starred reviews: *Publishers Weekly, School Library Journal*
- Goodreads Choice Award, Young Adult Fiction nominee, 2021
- Edgar Award for Best Young Adult nominee, 2022
- William C. Morris Award finalist, 2022
- Rainbow Book List Top Ten for Teen Readers, 2022
- Best Fiction for Young Adults, 2022
- Teens' Top Ten, 2022

Conversation Starters
1. In what ways do the experiences of Chiamaka and Devon showcase issues within modern society?
2. Do you think that as a society we are moving toward more racially motivated incidents like those at Niveus?
3. How does Àbíké-Íyímídé examine the issue of intersectionality and the difficulty it can pose for BIPOC (Black, Indigenous, people of color) youth? Is this an important concept to examine in high school classrooms?

All the Bad Apples by Moïra Fowley-Doyle. Kathy Dawson Books, 2019. (L)

Deena has grown up knowing all the women in her family are labeled *bad apples,* but after finding letters purporting to be from her older sister who supposedly jumped off a cliff, she gathers her friends to try to find her sister. While looking, they trace a path uncovering horrendous abuse that her ancestors faced.

Awards and Honors
- Starred review: *Booklist*
- Rise: A Feminist Book Project List, 2020

Conversation Starters
1. A lot of Irish history informs the plot. Did any of it surprise you?
2. Were you prepared for the revelation at the end about the letters?

As Far As You'll Take Me by Phil Stamper. Bloomsbury YA, 2021. (G)

Marty just has to get away from his small town and all of the small-minded people there, so he tells his parents that he got into a prestigious music program, packs up his oboe and the rest of his stuff, and arranges to stay in London with a relative. When he arrives, he quickly falls into a relationship with another musician, traveling all over Europe but somehow never finding time to practice. Eventually, his secrets are bound to come out.

Awards and Honors
- Starred review: *Booklist*

Conversation Starters

1. Can you run away from your secrets? What is a better way to handle Marty's issues?
2. Does Marty really want a music career?

Birthday by Meredith Russo. Macmillan/St. Martin's/Flatiron, 2019. (T)

Eric's and Morgan's families were thrust together the day they were born when they were all snowed in at the hospital thanks to a freak, out-of-season September blizzard that hit their Tennessee community. Over the course of six birthdays, their lives unfold in complex and beautiful ways.

Awards and Honors

- Starred review: *Booklist*
- New York Public Library's Top 10 Teen Books, 2019
- Goodreads Choice Award, Young Adult Fiction nominee, 2019
- Texas Library Association's TAYSHAS Reading List Top 10, 2020
- Rhode Island Teen Book Award nominee, 2021

Conversation Starters

1. Does the specific set of circumstances required for the families to meet initially (a blizzard in September in Tennessee) seem believable, or does it strain your credulity?
2. How did the format of the book, being one day a year, impact how much story was able to be told?

Cool for the Summer by Dahlia Adler. Wednesday Books, 2021. (Q)

Lara has had a crush on the same guy for the past three years; he's cute, and sweet, and is actually flirting with her now. But she can't get the girl she spent the summer with out of her head, and her summer fling is now a student at her school.

Awards and Honors

- Starred review: *Booklist*

Conversation Starters
  1. High school is a time when some youth learn who they really are.
     What can you think of that you learned about yourself in high school?
  2. How do you know if an attraction is just a crush?

Date Me, Bryson Keller by Kevin van Whye. Random House Books for Young Readers, 2020. (G)

The whole high school knows that Bryson Keller doesn't date, but he accepts a dare stating that he must say yes to the first person who asks him out on Monday morning. Kai Sheridan decides to try his luck, sure that Bryson will be willing to lose the dare instead of going out with another guy. To his surprise, Bryson accepts, under the idea that they'll fake-date to confuse everyone. But as the fake dates go on, Kai starts to feel like the fake just might be turning real.

Conversation Starters
  1. Can you name another book or movie that has this same premise?
  2. Have you ever taken a chance on a dare?

Death Prefers Blondes by Caleb Roehrig. Feiwel & Friends, 2019. (B, Q)

Margo gets her thrills by pulling off fashionable burglaries with her drag queen friends, but one night, everything changes, and now the group is forced to use their thievery and disguise skills just to survive.

Awards and Honors
  • Starred review: *Booklist*

Conversation Starters
  1. This book is frequently compared to *RuPaul's Drag Race* and *Ocean's 11*. Are these comparisons warranted? Why or why not?
  2. Does it hurt anyone if you shoplift small things?

The Feeling of Falling in Love by Mason Deaver. PUSH, 2022. (T, G)

Neil has to spend his spring break from boarding school with his family because his older brother is getting married. Right before he's set to leave, his friends-with-benefits/not-boyfriend Josh confesses that he's in love with Neil, so obviously Neil has to break it off. But Josh was set to go to the wedding with Neil, and he's going to be at the wedding anyway, so the only thing Neil can think to do is convince his roommate Wyatt to come to California for the wedding and pretend to be his date so that Josh will get jealous and move on. With fake dating, "and they were roommates," and "there was only one bed," what could possibly go wrong?

Conversation Starters
1. Is it difficult to use one set of pronouns for a person when you're with just them and another set for that person when you're around other people?
2. What do you notice about this love triangle?

Girl Crushed by Katie Heaney. Knopf Books for Young Readers, 2020. (L)

After suddenly becoming girlfriendless and best-friendless all at once, Quinn is feeling a little rudderless. But she sees the lead singer of a local band, Ruby, who herself has just ended a relationship, and starts to crush hard. And if Quinn can't be with her ex, Jamie, why not try things with Ruby?

Conversation Starters
1. Rebound relationships happen to pretty much everyone. What do you think will happen to this one?
2. Do you think this is a realistic plot setup? Why or why not?

How It All Blew Up by Arvin Ahmadi. Viking Books for Young Readers, 2020. (G)

The first thing you need to know about Amir is that despite his being in an airport interrogation room, it's not what it looks like. Yes, he's Iranian and Muslim, but it's not what you think. This is a different story. When he came out and everything fell apart, he ran away to Rome. He thinks things will be better in Italy, but they just get more complicated. And then he has to explain everything to US Customs.

Awards and Honors
- Starred review: *School Library Journal*

Conversation Starters
1. Have you ever wanted to run away to start over as a whole new you? What do you imagine the cost would be?
2. Do you have a secret? Something you love but are afraid to share for fear of ridicule or worse? How do you handle it?

How to Excavate a Heart by Jake Maia Arlow. HarperTeen, 2022. (L)

Shani is excited to be spending winter break of her first year at college doing an internship in Washington, DC, with her favorite paleoichthyologist, especially since she just got dumped by her girlfriend; but when one of her new roommates asks her to take over her dog-walking gig, the last person she expects to see is the cute girl Shani's mom hit with her car on the way into town.

Awards and Honors
- Starred review: *Kirkus Reviews*

Conversation Starters
1. What is the most ridiculous way to meet a potential romantic interest?
2. Are you surprised at the way this story turned out?

I Was Born for This by Alice Oseman. Scholastic, 2022. (T, G, A)

Angel lives and breathes her favorite boy band, The Ark, and plans to meet her best internet friend in London so they can go see The Ark's concert together. Jimmy is the front man of The Ark, dealing with anxiety, pressure, a new contract, and rumors that he's dating one of his bandmates.

Awards and Honors
- Starred review: *Kirkus Reviews*
- Goodreads Choice Award, Young Adult Fiction nominee, 2018 (original publication in the United Kingdom)
- Rainbow Book List, 2023

Conversation Starters
1. What do you do when you feel anxious?
2. What do you geek out over?

Indestructible Object by Mary McCoy. Simon & Schuster Books for Young Readers, 2021. (B)

Lee has been running a successful podcast with her boyfriend for two years, until he breaks up with her right after graduation, on air. To make matters worse, her parents also announce that they're splitting up. It's a lot all at once. So how does a podcaster process everything? By getting a few friends together and starting a podcast to investigate if love actually exists at all.

Awards and Honors
- Best Fiction for Young Adults, 2022

Conversation Starters
1. What are some ways that you cope when everything seems to be falling apart?
2. Is there another way you can think of to work through your problems?

Kissing Ezra Holtz (and Other Things I Did for Science) by Brianna R. Shrum. Sky Pony Press, 2019. (B)

Of course, Amalia's AP Psychology teacher pairs her up for a group project with the guy from her synagogue she's been avoiding her whole life. For their project, she and Ezra decide to bring back a study that suggests it can make any two people fall in love. As they refine their experiment on others, it might actually be working on them.

Conversation Starters

1. Do you think that the experiment Amalia and Ezra conduct would work in real life?
2. What does this book have to say about dealing with rejection and disappointment?

The Last True Poets of the Sea by Julia Drake. Little, Brown Books for Young Readers, 2019. (B)

When her brother Sam attempts to take his own life, Violet is sent to live in small-town Maine with her uncle, where she and her brother used to spend summers. She passes her time trying to unravel the mystery surrounding a shipwreck in which one of her ancestors was the only survivor and attempting to locate the wreck. When other local teens help her, she gets especially close to Liv.

Awards and Honors

• Starred reviews: *Booklist, Bulletin of the Center for Children's Books, Kirkus Reviews, Publishers Weekly, School Library Journal*

Conversation Starters

1. Are there any well-told stories from your family history that have become almost family myths or legends?
2. What kinds of comparisons can you draw between the wreckage of the ship and the wreckage of Sam's and Violet's lives?

Leah on the Offbeat by Becky Albertalli. Balzer + Bray, 2018. (B)

In a companion novel to *Simon vs. the Homo Sapiens Agenda,* this book follows Simon's friend Leah as the group of characters gets ready to graduate high school and go off to college. Everyone seems to be going off in their own directions, and couples are getting together and breaking up all over the place. When Simon came out, it was a big deal, but Leah doesn't know how to tell her friends she's bisexual. While she and Abby start planning on going to the same college and becoming roommates, there might be some other feelings developing.

Awards and Honors
- Starred reviews: *Booklist, Kirkus Reviews*

Conversation Starters
1. Would you go to a college just because your friends or your crush was going there?
2. Have you ever felt like a side character in your own life?

Let's Talk about Love by Claire Kann. Swoon Reads, 2018. (A, B)

Alice already knows that she's biromantic asexual, but when her girlfriend dumps her for being ace, Alice's summer plans revolve around binging her favorite shows, spending time with her best friends, and working at the library for rent money. She likes working at the library, but when they hire a new staffer named Takumi, her plans to swear off dating go out the window.

Awards and Honors
- Goodreads Choice Award, Young Adult Fiction nominee, 2018

Conversation Starters
1. Who do you think feels more left out, Alice, for being a third wheel to her friends, or her friends, when Alice starts dating Takumi?
2. What is the relationship between Alice and her family like? Is her asexuality a difficulty between Alice and her parents?

The Love and Lies of Rukhsana Ali by Sabina Khan. Scholastic, 2019. (L, G)

When Rukhsana's conservative Muslim parents find out she's dating a girl, they send her off to relatives in Bangladesh to find a nice Bengali boy to marry. While there, she learns more about her extended family, why her parents are so against her being a lesbian, and how destructive homophobia can be when she meets Sohail, a gay boy in Bangladesh.

Awards and Honors
- Starred review: *School Library Journal*

Conversation Starters
1. Khan contrasts Rukhsana's classmates and friends with her family, especially her extended family. Taken as a whole, are her parents and family deliberately harmful, or are they misguided?
2. How well do the events with Sohail fit with the rest of the plot?

Love, Creekwood by Becky Albertalli. Balzer + Bray, 2020. (G, B)

After Simon and Blue started dating in real life, and Leah and Abby had their night at prom, the characters from *Simon vs. the Homo Sapiens Agenda, The Upside of Unrequited,* and *Leah on the Offbeat* are all in college, navigating life over e-mail.

Conversation Starters
1. What changes when friends go from seeing each other every day in high school to being at different colleges?
2. How does the Creekwood crew navigate the changes between high school and college?

Loveless by Alice Oseman. Scholastic Press, 2022. (A, L, P)

Georgia is all set to start university with her two best friends, especially after an embarrassing incident at the prom after-party when it was revealed that she had never been kissed. Unfortunately, her friends Pip and Jason are in a different college at the university, and she has to share a room with Rooney, who quickly presses the three into forming a Shakespeare Society. University is about discovering who you are, and Georgia just might have all the right ingredients to figure out why she has faked having crushes and avoided kissing.

Awards and Honors
• Rainbow Book List Top Ten for Teen Readers, 2023

Conversation Starters
1. Which Shakespeare play is the gayest?
2. Have you ever thought that other people were joking about relationship stuff or finding people attractive?

Ophelia After All by Racquel Marie. Feiwel and Friends, 2022. (Q)

Ophelia is known by all as being obsessed with boys, possibly even more than her beloved roses. But she starts thinking less and less about a perfect prom with her ex-boyfriend and more about a cute girl named Talia. How can she reconcile the image that everyone else has of her with who she really is?

Awards and Honors
- Rainbow Book List, 2023

Conversation Starters
1. How do you cope when the image everyone has of you doesn't match up to who you really are?
2. How do people know you when you don't even know yourself? What happens when you figure out who you are?

Picture Us in the Light by Kelly Loy Gilbert. Little, Brown Books for Young Readers, 2018. (G)

Danny can't figure out what his parents, immigrants from China, are hiding. And while he just got accepted to his dream school, Rhode Island School of Design, something's wrong. It's almost the anniversary of his friend's suicide; he doesn't know how college will be without his best friend, Harry; his friend group is strained; and he's starting to develop more feelings for Harry.

Awards and Honors
- Starred reviews: *Booklist, Bulletin of the Center for Children's Books, Kirkus Reviews, Publishers Weekly, School Library Journal*
- California Book Award for Young Adult Gold, 2018
- Los Angeles Times Book Prize for Young Adult Literature nominee, 2018
- Stonewall Honor Book in Children's Literature, 2019

Conversation Starters
1. What lengths would you go to in order to achieve your goals?
2. Have you ever uncovered a secret and wished maybe you hadn't?

Stay Gold by Tobly McSmith. HarperTeen, 2020. (T)

Pony wants to spend his senior year passing at his new high school, and he plans to be as unnoticeable as possible. That plan meets an immediate roadblock when Pony and Georgia, a cheerleader who also wants to stay as under the radar as possible, see each other on the first day of the school year.

Awards and Honors
- Starred review: *School Library Journal*

Conversation Starters
1. Have you ever felt interested in someone you know you shouldn't?
2. What if you don't want anyone else to find out about your secret attraction?

That's Not What Happened by Kody Keplinger. Scholastic, 2018. (A)

Three years after a school shooting, Lee and the other survivors are still trying to come to terms with what happened. While Lee has to decide if she should tell the truth about the details surrounding her best friend's death, she also has to deal with what comes after high school and prom and how to explain to her friends that she is asexual.

Conversation Starters
1. Keplinger makes a choice in the book to avoid naming the shooter or making the story about the shooter. How does that contrast with media and news reports of real school shootings, and to what effect?
2. Lee struggles with wanting to tell the truth, both about her friend's death and her asexuality. In what ways do her fellow survivors' decisions on telling their truths impact her?

We Are Okay by Nina LaCour. Dutton Books for Young Readers, 2017. (L)

Marin lost her mother when she was young, never knew her father, and grew up with her grandfather, but when he dies suddenly, something in her breaks, and she bolts from California to her college in New York, leaving everyone behind without a word. But after fall semester ends and she's alone in the dorm over winter break, Marin has to face not only her best friend Mabel visiting but also the trauma she's been avoiding.

Awards and Honors
- Starred reviews: *Booklist, Kirkus Reviews, Publishers Weekly, School Library Journal*
- Goodreads Choice Award, Young Adult Fiction nominee, 2017
- Michael L. Printz Award, 2018
- Rhode Island Teen Book Award nominee, 2019
- Lincoln Award nominee, 2019

Conversation Starters
1. Has anything ever made you want to just leave everything behind?
2. Is this book more about grief or loneliness?

You Asked for Perfect by Laura Silverman. Sourcebooks Fire, 2019. (B)

Ariel is stressed out trying to make sure everything about his high school years is perfect so that he can get into the best college. But after failing a calculus quiz, he asks Amir to tutor him. Math may not be Ariel's thing, but Amir might be.

Awards and Honors
- Starred review: *VOYA*

Conversation Starters
1. How much pressure to be perfect do you feel from parents, family, teachers, and society in general?
2. Is perfection achievable, and what are the consequences of either striving for perfection or failing to be perfect?

You Should See Me in a Crown by Leah Johnson. Scholastic Press, 2020. (B)

Liz desperately wants to get out of her small town, to go to a prestigious college, join an orchestra, and become a doctor. She has the grades for it but needs financial aid to be able to pay to go to her dream school. When the aid she's counting on disappears, her last shot at her dream is to run for prom queen, because winning comes with a scholarship. It's the last thing in the world she really wants to do, especially when the new girl, Mack, is running as well.

Awards and Honors
- Starred reviews: *Kirkus Reviews, Publishers Weekly*
- Goodreads Choice Award, Young Adult Fiction nominee, 2020
- Swoon Award, Young Adult Romance, 2020
- Top Ten Quick Picks for Reluctant Young Adult Readers, 2021
- Rainbow Book List Top Ten for Teen Readers, 2021
- Stonewall Honor Book in Children's Literature, 2021
- Rhode Island Teen Book Award nominee, 2022

Conversation Starters
1. What message does it send when the only way a Black girl can get a scholarship to go to her first-choice college is to not only enter but win a competition that is based on looks and popularity?
2. What would you do to get an elusive scholarship you really needed?

SCIENCE FICTION

Gideon the Ninth by Tamsyn Muir. Tor, 2019. (L)

When the Emperor summons the heirs of each of the solar system's Houses to a necromantic trial of wits and skill, Harrowhark Nonagesimus forces Gideon to accompany her as her cavalier. If Harrowhark succeeds, she'll become immortal—but without Gideon's sword, she'll fail, and the Ninth House will die with her. Then dead bodies start turning up. Can Gideon and Harrow stay alive long enough to solve the Emperor's puzzle?

Awards and Honors
- Starred reviews: *Booklist, Kirkus Reviews, Publishers Weekly*
- Goodreads Choice Award, Science Fiction nominee and Debut Novel nominee, 2019
- BookNest Award for Best Debut Novel nominee, 2019
- Locus Award, 2020
- Crawford Award, 2020

- Hugo Award finalist, 2020
- Nebula Award finalist, 2020
- Dragon Award finalist, 2020
- World Fantasy Award finalist, 2020
- British Fantasy Award, Best Newcomer (Sydney J. Bounds Award) nominee, 2020

Conversation Starters

1. Does this book fall into the bury-your-gays trope, and if so, does it count when necromancers are involved?
2. There are a lot of twists and turns throughout the story. Do they make it hard to understand what is going on?

The Last 8 by Laura Pohl. Sourcebooks Fire, 2019. (A, Q)

The First 7 by Laura Pohl. Sourcebooks Fire, 2020. (A, Q)

Clover somehow survives the alien invasion that kills off, to the best of her knowledge, everyone else. Luckily, her abuelo taught her how to fly, and she hopes that if she flies far enough, maybe she'll find another survivor. Eventually, she comes across a radio signal telling her to come to Area 51 and that she's not alone. There are other teenagers still alive, and she's one of the last eight. They may not be a team of heroes, but they're all that's left, and they're trying to stick together. And that's when she accidentally discovers a space-ship hidden on base.

In *The First 7,* Clover and her found family/friends have gotten the ship to work and are exploring the galaxy when they receive a distress signal from Earth. Are there more survivors?

Conversation Starters

1. What would you do to survive in this situation?
2. If you and your friends have managed to survive an alien invasion and are safe, would you return to earth to potentially save someone else? Why or why not?

Once and Future by A. R. Capetta and Cory McCarthy.
Jimmy Patterson, 2019. (Q)

Sword in the Stars by A. R. Capetta and Cory McCarthy.
Jimmy Patterson, 2020. (Q)

In a retelling of Arthurian legend set in the future and in
space, a teenage Merlin attempts to corral Ari Helix and her
friends as they fight an intergalactic corporation.

In the sequel to *Once and Future,* Ari, Merlin, and their
pals have been trapped in the Middle Ages, looking for the
Holy Grail that might take down the Mercer Corporation
permanently.

Awards and Honors

- Starred reviews, *Once and Future*: *Kirkus Reviews, Publishers Weekly, School Library Journal*
- Starred reviews, *Sword in the Stars*: *School Library Journal*
- *Once and Future*: Rise: A Feminist Book Project List, 2020

Conversation Starters

1. One of the themes common in Arthurian legend is rebellion against tradition in an attempt to make things better and fairer. What message does one get when the story is set against a corporate empire?
2. The world that Ari and her friends live in is exceedingly queer normative. How does that impact one's reading of the book?
3. Time travel can make even the simplest of stories complicated. In what ways did the time travel in this book impact the plot and the characters?
4. While our characters started out in the first book with fairly queer-normative societies, going back to a historical/legendary period from the first of the Arthurs shows a marked difference. What similarities and differences can you identify?

They Both Die at the End by Adam Silvera. **Quill Tree Books, 2017. (G, B)**

In a future where a company knows when everyone will die, Matteo and
Rufus meet because they have the same death date. The boys don't know
how or exactly when, but by the end of the day, they'll both be dead. So,
what do two teenagers who know they're going to die do on their last day?

Awards and Honors
- Starred reviews: *Booklist, Kirkus Reviews, Publishers Weekly, School Library Journal*
- Goodreads Choice Award, Young Adult Fiction nominee, 2017
- Lincoln Award, 2020
- Flicker Tale Children's Book Award for Older Readers, 2021

Conversation Starters
1. What would you do if you knew you were going to die by the end of the day?
2. Would you rather know when you'll die or not know?
3. Were you expecting a different ending, based on the title?

SPECULATIVE FICTION

Super Adjacent by Crystal Cestari. Little, Brown Books for Young Readers, 2020. (L)

Claire has been a major fan of superheroes all of her life, so when she manages to get an internship with a group of superheroes in Chicago, she's ecstatic. It doesn't hurt that the newest hero is pretty cute. And then there's Bridgette, who is tired of being stuck in the role of "girlfriend of a superhero." But then the heroes go missing. Can Claire and Bridgette rescue them?

Awards and Honors
- Starred review: *School Library Journal*

Conversation Starters
1. What makes someone a hero or heroic?
2. What one quality would you possess if you were a superhero? How would it benefit others?

***When We Were Magic* by Sarah Gailey. Simon & Schuster Books for Young Readers, 2020. (B)**

With possibly one of the most surprising opening scenes in young adult literature, *When We Were Magic* follows a group of teen witches as they attempt to make things right after the accidental murder of a classmate.

Conversation Starters
1. The title places the group's magic in the past tense. Does this make sense with the plot and actions in the book?
2. Can a coven become a found family?

ACTIVITIES, PROJECTS, AND PROGRAMS FOR OLDER TEENS

Queer Prom

Some schools and areas offer a queer prom, but not everywhere, and not all schools allow same-sex couples or gender-nonconforming attire. If you're able, try offering one. The most important thing is to find a location that will be a safe space. Advertisement will be important, keeping in mind that sometimes posters with LGBTQIA+ themes are defaced and subtly threaten youth who would otherwise consider attending. Consider social media as an alternative. Music should be easy with all the sound systems around today! Refreshments can be done many ways—potluck, sign-up, catered in—all of which will depend on how much money is in the budget. A subject that also needs to be considered is security. No one wants some disruptive group barging in or causing trouble in the parking lot. Even though this is a lot of work, attending a queer prom may turn out to be the best memory of their teenage years! This program goes well with *The Prom: A Novel Based on the Hit Broadway Musical* (annotated in chapter 4).

Banned Book Club

Because so many of the titles that have been banned or challenged recently have LGBTQIA+ content, teens who are LGBTQIA+ might have a special interest in reading banned books. Later, the group may branch out into activism, contacting local elected officials about issues of censorship and free speech or supporting school or public librarians in their areas who are facing book challenges. A number of the books in this chapter have been challenged or banned in numerous places, so a good starting place for a banned book club would be *Gender Queer* or *All Boys Aren't Blue*.

Henna Art

Henna can be wonderful for self-expression. See if there's a local henna artist in your community who is willing to come in, talk about the art form, and do designs for your teens. This pairs wonderfully with *The Henna Wars* (annotated in chapter 4) and *The Love and Lies of Rukhsana Ali*.

Clothing Drive

Ask your teens if they would like to do a clothing drive. This is an activity all teens could take part in. Query the LGBTQIA+ teens you know and ask them to be part of the committee spearheading the drive. Assist them in working out such details as the following:

- What will ultimately be done with the clothes?
- Do you want a clothing drive, possibly for teens experiencing poverty or housing insecurity, or a clothing swap, primarily for transgender and nonbinary teens to expand their wardrobe with pieces that match their gender identity and expression?
- Again, advertising will be essential, so what kind of advertising do you want to do?
- What time of the year will yield the most involvement? Check local school calendars for optimum times.
- When and where do you want to hold the event?
- What are other ways to get youth involved?

Be sure to do exit surveys and ask what other activities your teens would like to see or what clubs they would like to have. In time, these activities can lead to a larger support community.

WRAP-UP

Even with all the book challenges and bans, most teens have the ability to get the books they want to read. If you work in a school that doesn't have a title because it's been banned or challenged, see if you can refer your students to the local public library. Many libraries have e-books, and they will also try to honor book requests, either through purchasing titles or requesting them through interlibrary loan. Book stores carry popular books, and Little Free Libraries can be created in multiple locations in a community to hold challenged books for free choosing and sharing.

NOTES

1. "Our Issue," True Colors United, https://truecolorsunited.org/our-issue/.
2. "Missed Opportunities: Youth Homelessness in America," Voices of Youth Count, under Finding 5, https://voicesofyouthcount.org/brief/national -estimates-of-youth-homelessness/.
3. The Trevor Project, *Homelessness and Housing Instability among LGBTQ Youth* (West Hollywood, CA: The Trevor Project, February 3, 2022), www.thetrevor project.org/research-briefs/homelessness-and-housing-instability-among-lgbtq -youth-feb-2022/.
4. "Street Transvestite Action Revolutionaries (STAR) Research Guide" (Lib-Guides at Pratt Institute), Pratt Institute Libraries, last updated January 27, 2023, https://libguides.pratt.edu/star.

What Teachers and Librarians Can Do to Support LGBTQIA+ Students

W e can show that our classrooms and libraries are safe spaces. We can put up rainbow and other pride flags. We can share our pronouns, and ask our students and patrons for theirs if they want to share them. We can ask them if they want us to use different names or pronouns for them when speaking with others, including their parents, because some teens may be more comfortable in one space than another. If we don't know what someone's pronouns are, we can use inclusive, gender-neutral language to refer to them. We can wear pins that affirm that our classrooms and libraries are welcoming. And we can have a diverse collection of books on our shelves so all of our young people can feel seen.

||||||||||||||||||||||

Voices from the Stacks
Kit Ballenger

At Pride and Less Prejudice, we provide free bundles of LGBTQIA+ books to pre-K through third grade classrooms across the United States and Canada to help young readers see themselves, their loved ones, and their friends reflected in stories. In our first three years, we've shared more than 6,000 picture books with over 3,000 educators, plus teaching guides and virtual workshops to support our community. The demand is staggering—at this point we're receiving several hundred requests every month!—and the positive feedback we hear from teachers and librarians about the impact of these stories on their classrooms is such an affirmation of the organization's mission. By sharing authentic stories reflecting a wide range of queer experiences, these books help educators foster safe spaces for their students, regardless of identity. And as schools and communities continue to challenge books with LGBTQIA+ themes and characters, we appreciate how important it is to get every single one of these books in the hands of young readers.

Sam Harris, the library director at the Charles Wright Academy in Tacoma, Washington, was quoted in *School Library Journal* as saying, "Wherever [students in the LGBTQIA+ community] are in their journey, they know this is a place where they'll be seen for their authentic selves."[1] Similarly, Tyler Sainato, school librarian at Caine Ridge High School in Antioch, Tennessee, says,

> I really do believe that this work can save lives. I feel like it is part of my purpose to amplify voices that are not heard often. My role in that is to provide a safe space where people can find books or other information where they can see themselves represented.[2]

And we can make sure that we have books on our shelves that reflect our students' and patrons' identities and lives, and that we don't restrict displaying them to the month of June for Rainbow Book Month. Queer books can be displayed year-round, in any displays. We don't highlight books by Black authors or about Black characters only in February for Black History Month. The same should be true about queer books.

||||||||||||||||||||||||

Ways to Promote Queer Literature in Schools

We all know that Pride is in June, but this can be problematic for school librarians because most schools are closing down for the summer in June. Books are being returned and inventory is being done. How can school librarians promote queer literature in other ways? Here are some ideas that don't involve Pride or June!

Celebrate Pride in December! Why should Christmas in July get all the action? Make a display of queer literature and create a clever caption for it, like "It's Always a Good Time to Celebrate Pride."

Do presentations to student clubs in your buildings. Most schools have GSAs (Gay-Straight Alliances) or social justice clubs or diversity clubs. Invite them into the library after school or before school or during lunch for a book talk (and serve snacks!).

Integrate queer titles into genre studies. Doing a talk on science fiction? Include Eliot Schrefer's *The Darkness Outside Us* (Katherine Tegen Books, 2021). Doing a mystery fiction talk? Include Kyle Lukoff's *Too Bright to See* (annotated in chapter 3). Queer literature crosses all genres and goes far beyond coming-out stories.

Include queer titles in summer reading lists. Many schools have summer reading lists, with books that are either voluntary or required. Integrate queer literature titles into those lists.

Participate in a book fair. Have "Diverse Books" displays at book fairs and include queer titles.

Celebrate the birthdays of queer icons (e.g., Harvey Milk) and create book displays to honor them.

Recognize that queer history is rich and diverse. You can integrate queer titles into other celebrations. What Black History Month celebration would be complete without books about people like Marsha Johnson or Barbara Jordan or James Baldwin? Include books by Malinda Lo during Asian American and Pacific Islander Heritage Month.

Make queer content discoverable. When cataloging your books, make sure MARC records reflect queer content in your online catalog. Not every child will feel comfortable asking you or another adult for these books, so find ways to provide multiple access points in your online catalog, including the use of subject headings, controlled vocabulary, and natural language.

Make queer content approachable for all. When you are book-talking queer titles, focus on commonalities between queer kids and their straight classmates when promoting books. Most kids deal with issues like crushes, family problems, bullying, and friendship. Building on the ways in which kids are alike will build empathy and help open the minds of straight kids toward reading books that feature the lives of queer students.

Post "safe space" stickers within easy view of students and staff. This will let queer kids know that they are welcome to come to the library.

Help build allies for queer kids and queer literature by preparing resource lists for colleagues containing queer titles.

Lead and participate in professional workshops for staff in your district.

—DAVE SAIA

Finally, everyone should remember CAPE TWIRL (see figure 6.1).

FIGURE 6.1
CAPE TWIRL

CIRCUMSTANCES: Parents/families aren't always safe for kids; let them tell you what can be shared with family members, and what name and/or pronouns to use and when.

ADVOCATE FOR YOUR COMMUNITY: Move away from asking/requiring gender on application forms, ask students or patrons if they want to share their pronouns and/or preferred name, and, if possible, provide gender neutral restrooms.

PROACTIVE: Have defenses prepared for any materials or policies that might be challenged.

EMBRACE differences.

TRAUMA-INFORMED: Watch out for signs of mental health issues and housing and food insecurity.

WELCOMING: Let children and young people know that you work in a safe space, and they are welcome.

INCLUSIVE: Be inclusive and make sure you show others that you're inclusive.

RESOURCES: Provide resources, and know the limitations of your resources.

CAPE TWIRL

LET kids be themselves!

NOTES

1. Quoted in Marva Hinton, "You've Got a Friend in Me," *School Library Journal,* June 2022, 27.
2. Quoted in Hinton, "You've Got a Friend in Me," 28.

APPENDIX A

Recommended Resources

Challenged and Banned Books Resources and Information

"Book Challenges by the Numbers" (infographic, p. 2). ALA Office for Intellectual Freedom, 2016. www.ala.org/advocacy/sites/ala.org .advocacy/files/content/Top%20Ten%20for%202016.pdf.

Carlisle, Madeleine. "'Gender Queer' Author 'Relieved' after Court Rules Book's Sale Can't Be Restricted in Virginia." *Time,* August 31, 2022. https://time.com/6210087/gender-queer-book-ban-maia-kobabe/.

"Censorship by the Numbers" (infographic). ALA Office for Intellectual Freedom, 2017. www.ala.org/advocacy/sites/ala.org.advocacy/files/ content/OIF%20Infographic%20-%20June%20-%20Page%202_0.pdf.

"Censorship by the Numbers" (infographic). ALA Office for Intellectual Freedom, 2018. www.ala.org/advocacy/sites/ala.org.advocacy/files/ content/2018-bbooks-graphic-1_0.jpg.

"Censorship by the Numbers, 2019" (infographic). ALA Office for Intellectual Freedom, 2019. www.ala.org/advocacy/sites/ala.org .advocacy/files/content/Censorship%20by%20the%20Numbers%20 2019_0_0.pdf.

"Censorship by the Numbers, 2020." ALA Office for Intellectual Freedom. https://alair.ala.org/handle/11213/16720.

"Free Downloads: Celebrate Banned Books Week." Banned and Challenged Books (website). ALA Office for Intellectual Freedom. www.ala.org/advocacy/bbooks/bannedbooksweek/ideasand resources/freedownloads.

Friedman, Johnathan, and Nadine Farid Johnson. *Banned in the USA: Rising School Book Bans Threaten Free Expression and Students' First Amendment Rights (April 2022).* PEN America, September 14, 2022. https://pen.org/banned-in-the-usa/.

Office for Intellectual Freedom, American Library Association. www.ala.org/aboutala/offices/oif.

"PEN America's Index of School Book Bans (July 1, 2021–June 30, 2022)." Google Sheets. https://docs.google.com/spreadsheets/d/1hTs_PB7Ku TMBtNMESFEGuK-0abzhNxVv4tgpI5-iKe8/edit?usp=sharing.

Rogerson, Karis. "How LGBTQIA+ Book Bans Impact Kids and Teens." *We Need Diverse Books* (blog), March 25, 2022. https://diversebooks.org/how-lgbtqia-book-bans-impact-kids-and-teens/.

"Top Ten Most Challenged Books Lists." Banned and Challenged Books (website). ALA Office for Intellectual Freedom. www.ala.org/advocacy/bbooks/frequentlychallengedbooks/top10.

Wood, Sarah. "Book Bans: What to Know." *US News,* May 17, 2022. www.usnews.com/education/k12/articles/book-bans-what-to-know.

Diversity Statistics

"CCBC Diversity Statistics." Cooperative Children's Book Center. https://ccbc.education.wisc.edu/literature-resources/ccbc-diversity-statistics/.

"CCBC Diversity Statistics Book Search." Cooperative Children's Book Center. https://ccbc.education.wisc.edu/diversity-statistics-book-search/.

"CCBC 2017 Statistics on LGBTQ+ Literature for Children and Teens." Cooperative Children's Book Center, April 6, 2018. https://ccbc.education.wisc.edu/ccbc-2017-statistics-on-lgbtq-literature-for-children-teens/.

Tyner, Madeline. "The CCBC's Diversity Statistics: Spotlight on LGBTQ+ Stories." *The Horn Book,* November 15, 2018. www.hbook.com/story/ccbcs-diversity-statistics-spotlight-lgbtq-stories.

Finding LGBTQIA+ Books

LGBTQ Reads. https://lgbtqreads.com.

Rainbow Round Table, American Library Association. www.ala.org/rt/rrt.

Stonewall Book Awards List. www.ala.org/rt/rrt/award/stonewall/ honored.

2016 Rainbow Book List. https://glbtrt.ala.org/rainbowbooks/archives/ 1207.

2017 Rainbow Book List. https://glbtrt.ala.org/rainbowbooks/archives/ 1255.

2018 Rainbow Book List. https://glbtrt.ala.org/rainbowbooks/archives/ 1270.

2019 Rainbow Book List. https://glbtrt.ala.org/rainbowbooks/archives/ 1324.

2020 Rainbow Book List. https://glbtrt.ala.org/rainbowbooks/archives/ 1331.

2021 Rainbow Book List. https://glbtrt.ala.org/rainbowbooks/archives/ 1341.

2022 Rainbow Book List. https://glbtrt.ala.org/rainbowbooks/archives/ 1429.

General References

Asexual Visibility and Education Network. https://asexuality.org.

Gender Wiki. https://gender.fandom.com/wiki/Gender_Wiki.

GLAAD. "Glossary of Terms: LGBTQ." In *GLAAD Media Reference Guide,* 11th ed. www.glaad.org/reference/terms.

Human Rights Campaign. "Glossary of Terms." www.hrc.org/resources/ glossary-of-terms.

Nonbinary Wiki. https://nonbinary.wiki/wiki/Main_Page.

Pride and Less Prejudice. www.prideandlessprejudice.org.

Wamsley, Laura. "A Guide to Gender Identity Terms." NPR, June 2, 2021. www.npr.org/2021/06/02/996319297/gender-identity-pronouns -expression-guide-lgbtq.

Homelessness Information

Ali Forney Center. www.aliforneycenter.org.

"The Cost of Coming Out: LGBT Youth Homelessness." Lesley University. https://lesley.edu/article/the-cost-of-coming-out-lgbt-youth -homelessness.

Covenant House (LGBTQ+ Youth and Gay Homelessness Shelter). www.covenanthouse.org/homeless-issues/lgbtq-homeless-youth.

"Homelessness and Housing." Youth.gov. https://youth.gov/youth-topics/ lgbtq-youth/homelessness.

"LGBTQ Youth Experiencing Homelessness." National Center for Homeless Education. https://nche.ed.gov/lgbtq-youth.

"Working with Homeless LGBTQ Youth." Lambda Legal. www.lamb dalegal.org/know-your-rights/article/youth-homeless.

Legal Resources

American Civil Liberties Union. www.aclu.org.

Lambda Legal. www.lambdalegal.org.

Sylvia Rivera Law Project. https://srlp.org.

Transgender Law Center. https://transgenderlawcenter.org.

Mental Health Information

Gonzalez, Oriana. "Multiracial LGBTQ Youth More Likely to Consider Suicide, Report Finds." Axios Health, August 11, 2022. www.axios .com/2022/08/11/lgbtq-multiracial-mental-health-trevor-project.

Trevor Project. *National Survey on LGBTQ Youth Mental Health.* West Hollywood, CA: The Trevor Project, 2021. www.thetrevorproject.org/survey-2021.

Trevor Project. *2022 National Survey on LGBTQ Youth Mental Health.* West Hollywood, CA: The Trevor Project, 2022. www.thetrevor 3project.org/survey-2022/.

Resources for Allies

"LGTBQ+ Youth Homelessness." National Network for Youth. https://nn4youth.org/lgbtq-homeless-youth.

PFLAG. https://pflag.org.

Safe Zone Project. https://thesafezoneproject.com.

Resources for the LGBTQIA+ Community

Asexual Visibility and Education Network. https://asexuality.org.

GLAAD. www.glaad.org.

GLSEN. www.glsen.org.

Human Rights Campaign. www.hrc.org.

interACT. https://interactadvocates.org.

Intersex Campaign for Equality. www.intersexequality.com.

National Center for Lesbian Rights. www.nclrights.org.

National Center for Transgender Equality. https://transequality.org.

Trans Lifeline. https://translifeline.org.

Trevor Project. www.thetrevorproject.org.

APPENDIX B

Authors and Illustrators to Know

Àbíké-Íyímídé, Faridah: www.faridahabikeiyimide.com, Twitter/Instagram: @faridahlikestea

Adeyoha, Angel: http://integratetheveil.com, Twitter: @angeladeyoha, Instagram: @adeyoha

Adeyoha, Koja: Instagram: @kojaadeyoha

Adler, Dahlia: www.dahliaadler.com, Twitter/Instagram: @MissDahlELama

Ahmadi, Arvin: www.arvinahmadi.com, Twitter/Instagram: @arvinahmadi

Albee, Jay: www.jenbreach.com, Twitter/Instagram: @jenbreach

Albertalli, Becky: www.beckyalbertalli.com, Twitter/Instagram: @becky albertalli

Alexander, Damian: https://damianimated.com, Twitter/Instagram: @DamiAnimated

Ancrum, K.: https://kancrum.com, Twitter: @KaylaAncrum, Instagram: @k.ancrum

Ang, Hui Qing: Twitter: @BurdHQ, Instagram: @chickensaredoodling

Arlow, Jake Maia: www.jakewhosagirl.com, Twitter/Instagram: @jakewhosa girl

Axelrod, Jadzia: www.jaredaxelrod.com, Twitter/Instagram: @planetx

Ayala-Kronos, Chris: www.harpercollins.com/blogs/authors/chris-ayala -kronos-20211228420106

Bailar, Schuyler: www.pinkmantaray.com, Twitter: @sb_pinkmantaray, Instagram: @pinkmantaray

Barnes, Elly: www.penguinrandomhouse.com/authors/2273711/elly-barnes

Bashardoust, Melissa: www.melissabashardoust.com

Bayron, Kalynn: www.kalynnbayron.com, Twitter/Instagram: @KalynnBayron

Bechdel, Alison: https://dykestowatchoutfor.com, Twitter: @AlisonBechdel

Berquist, Emma: www.emmaberquist.com, Twitter/Instagram: @eeberquist

Bigelow, Lisa Jenn: https://lisajennbigelow.com, Twitter/Instagram: @LisaJennBigelow

Blais, Mykaell: www.penguinrandomhouse.com/authors/2255682/ mykaell-blais

Blake, Ashley Herring: www.ashleyherringblake.com, Twitter/Instagram: @ashleyhblake

Blas, Terry: www.terryblas.com, Twitter/Instagram: @TerryBlas

Bongiovanni, Archie: www.archiebongiovanni.com, Twitter: @grease_bat, Instagram: @babywrist

Borinsky, Agnes: www.rustchukfarm.org

Bowman, Akemi Dawn: www.akemidawnbowman.com, Twitter/Instagram: @AkemiDawnBowman

Brueggemann, Wibke: www.wibkebrueggemann.com, Twitter/Instagram: @WibkeBrueggeman

Bulla, Michael Gray: http://michaelgraybulla.com, Twitter/Instagram: @graybulla

Bunker, Lisa: www.lisabunker.net, Twitter: @LisaBunker

Burgess, Matthew: www.matthewjohnburgess.com, Twitter/Instagram: @MatthewBurgessJ

Burgess, Rebecca: www.rebeccaburgess.co.uk, Twitter/Instagram: @theorahart

Caldwell, Stella: Instagram: @stellacaldwell

Callender, Kacen: www.kacencallender.com, Twitter: @kacencallender

Capetta, A. R.: https://onceandfuturestories.com, Instagram: @ar_capetta

Cathro, Robbie: www.robbiecathro.com, Twitter/Instagram: @RobbieCathro

Ceilley, Mark: https://markceilley.com, Twitter: @MarkCeilley

Cestari, Crystal: www.crystalcestari.com, Twitter/Instagram: @crystalcestari

Chanani, Nidhi: https://everydayloveart.com, Twitter/Instagram: @nidhiart

Charlton-Trujillo, e. E.: www.eecharlton-trujillo.com, Twitter/Instagram: @pinatadirector

Chu, Wesley: https://wesleychu.com, Twitter: @wes_chu, Instagram: @wesleychu1

Chua, Charlene: https://charlenechua.com, Twitter/Instagram: @charlenedraws

Clare, Cassandra: https://cassandraclare.com, Twitter: @cassieclare

Clifton-Brown, Holly: http://hollycliftonbrown.blogspot.com, Twitter: @HollyRCB, Instagram: @hollycliftonbrownillustration

Foley, Tim: https://timfoleyillustration.com

Ford, J. R.: www.jrandvanessaford.com/calvin, Twitter: @MrJRFord

Ford, Vanessa: www.jrandvanessaford.com/calvin, Twitter: @VanessaFordDC

Forman, Gayle: www.gayleforman.com, Twitter/Instagram: @gayleforman

Fowley-Doyle, Moïra: https://moirafowley.com

Fry, Kate: www.orcabook.com/ContributorInfo?ContribId=854

Gailey, Sarah: https://sarahgailey.com, Twitter: @gaileyfrey

Gale, Heather: https://heathergale.net, Twitter/Instagram: @writergale

Garden, Nancy: https://us.macmillan.com/author/nancygarden

Garrett, Camryn: www.camryngarrett.com, Twitter: @dancingofpens, Instagram: @camryngwrites

Gilbert, Kelly Loy: https://kellyloygilbert.weebly.com, Twitter/Instagram: @KellyLoyGilbert

Gino, Alex: www.alexgino.com, Twitter: @lxgino

Gow, Robin: https://robingow.com,Twitter: @gow_robin_frank, Instagram: @rockin_robin_1

Grant, Mira: www.miragrant.com, Twitter: @miragrant; *See also* McGuire, Seanan

Gravel, Elise: http://elisegravel.com/en/, Twitter: @EliseGravel, Instagram: @elise_gravel

Gregorio, I. W.: www.iwgregorio.com, Twitter/Instagram: @IWGregorio

Grimm, Gavin: Twitter: @GavinGrimmVA

Hancox, Lewis: Twitter: @LewisHancox, Instagram, TikTok: @lewishancox films

Harren, Kayla: www.kaylaharren.com, Instagram: @kaylaharren

Hastings, Levi: www.levihastings.com, Twitter/Instagram: @LeviHastingsArt

Hawkins, Rachel: www.rachelhawkinsbooks.com, Twitter/Instagram: @ladyhawkins

Heaney, Katie: www.katieheaney.com, Twitter: @KTHeaney, Instagram: @katieheaney

Helena, Larissa: Twitter: @larilena

Hernandez, Will: Instagram: @willhernandezdraws

Herriot, Lindsay: www.orcabook.com/ContributorInfo?ContribId=924

Hillman, Jonathan: www.jhillmanbooks.com, Twitter/Instagram: @jhillman books

Horne, Maggie: https://maggiehorne.com, Twitter/Instagram: @MaggieHas Hornes

Hulme, Jay: https://jayhulme.com, Twitter/Instagram: @JayHulmePoet

Jaigirdar, Adiba: https://adibajaigirdar.com, Twitter: @adiba_j, Instagram: @dibs_j

Jasinska, Alicia: http://aliciajasinska.com, Twitter: @aliciajasinska, Instagram: @aliciamja

Jimerson, Tristan: www.simonandschuster.com/authors/Tristan-Jimerson/ 141045828

John, Cathryn: Instagram: @flo.studios

Johnson, George M.: https://iamgmjohnson.com, Twitter/Instagram: @IamGMJohnson

Johnson, Leah: www.byleahjohnson.com, Twitter/Instagram: @byleahjohnson

Johnston, E. K.: www.ekjohnston.ca, Twitter: @ek_johnston

Juanita, Kaylani: http://kaylanijuanita.com, Twitter/Instagram: @kaylanijuanita

Kaban, Eda: www.edakaban.com, Twitter/Instagram: @petiteturk

Kann, Claire: www.clairekann.com, Twitter/Instagram: @KannClaire

Karlsson, Adria: www.adriakarlsson.com, Twitter/Instagram: @adriakarlsson

Kearney, Rob: www.robkearneystrongman.com, Instagram: @worlds_strongest _gay

Keplinger, Kody: http://kodykeplinger.com, Twitter: @Kody_Keplinger, Instagram: @kodykeplinger

Khan, Sabina: https://sabina-khan.com, Twitter/Instagram: @Sabina_Writer

Kirk, Sam: http://iamsamkirk.com, Twitter/Instagram: @iamsamkirk

Kobabe, Maia: https://redgoldsparkspress.com, Instagram: @redgoldsparks

Konigsberg, Bill: https://billkonigsberg.com, Twitter: @billkonigsberg, Instagram: @bkonigsberg

Kutub, Naz: https://nazkutub.com, Twitter/Instagram: @nazkutub

La Sala, Ryan: www.ryanlasala.com, Twitter/Instagram: @theryanlasala

Laberis, Stephanie: https://stephlaberis.squarespace.com, Twitter: @Steph Laberis, Instagram: @steph_laberis

LaCour, Nina: www.ninalacour.com, Twitter/Instagram: @nina_lacour

Latimer, E.: www.elatimer.com, Twitter/Instagram: @ELatimerWrites

Layne, Aliza: https://alizalayne.com, Twitter: @alizabees, Instagram: @aliza layne

Leali, Michael: https://michaelleali.com, Twitter: @michaelleali

Lee, Emery: www.emeryleebooks.com, Twitter/TikTok: @EmeryLeeWho, Instagram: @emeryleebooks

Lee, Lyla: https://lylaleebooks.com, Twitter/Instagram: @literarylyla

Lee, Mackenzi, www.mackenzilee.com, Instagram: @themackenzilee

Levithan, David: www.davidlevithan.com

Lil Miss Hot Mess: www.lilmisshotmess.com, Twitter/Instagram: @LilMiss
HotMess

Lo, Malinda: www.malindalo.com, Twitter/Instagram: @malindalo

Locke, Katherine: www.katherinelockebooks.com, Twitter/Instagram: 7
@bibliogato

Lockington, Mariama J.: Twitter: @marilock, Instagram: @forblackgirlslikeme

London, Alex: www.calexanderlondon.com, Twitter: @ca_london, Instagram:
@alexander_london

Lorinczi, Balazs: Twitter: @balakinlb

Love, Jessica: https://jesslove.format.com, Instagram: @jesslovedraws

Lozano, Luciano: https://lucianolozano.com, Instagram: @ilustrista

Lukoff, Kyle: www.kylelukoff.com, Twitter: @kylelukoff, Instagram:
@kylelukoffwrites

Lundin, Britta: www.brittalundin.com, Twitter: @brittashipsit, Instagram:
@britta_lundin

Madison, Megan: https://meganpamelaruthmadison.wordpress.com, Twitter:
@meganprmadison, Instagram: @meganmadison

Marie, Racquel: https://racquelmariebooks.squarespace.com, Twitter: @blonde
withabook, Instagram: @blonde_with_a_book

Martins, Vitor: https://vitormartins.blog/, Twitter/Instagram: @vitormrtns

Mays, Nancy K.: Twitter: @nkmays

McCarthy, Cory: https://onceandfuturestories.com, Twitter: @CoriMccarthy,
Instagram: @cory__mccarthy

McClintick, Joanna: www.joannamcclintick.com, Twitter: @jmc_clintick,
Instagram: @jkmcclintick1

McCoy, Mary: http://mary-mccoy.com, Twitter/Instagram: @MaryElMcCoy

McGillis, Holly: Twitter/Instagram: @hollymcgillis

McGuire, C. M.: www.seeemmcguire.com, Twitter/Instagram: @SeeEmMcGuire

McGuire, Seanan: www.seananmcguire.com, Twitter/Instagram: @seanan
mcguire

McLaughlin, Julie: www.whatwouldjuliedraw.com, Instagram: @juliebot

McLemore, Anna-Marie: http://author.annamariemclemore.com/p/welcome.html,
Twitter: @LaAnnaMarie

McSmith, Tobly: www.bobandtobly.com, Twitter/Instagram: @toblymcsmith

medina: https://www.levinequerido.com/medina

Medina, Juana: www.juanamedina.com, Twitter: @juanamedina, Instagram:
@juana_medina

Medina, Nico: Twitter: @nicomedina, Instagram: @duh_nico

Mejia, Tehlor Kay: www.tehlorkaymejia.com, Twitter/Instagram: @tehlorkay

Membrino, Anna: www.annamembrinobooks.com, Twitter: @annamembo

Mihaly, Christy: www.christymihaly.com, Twitter: @CMwriter4kids, Instagram: @christymihaly

Miller, Linsey: www.linseymiller.com, Twitter: @LinseyMiller, Instagram:
@linsey.miller

Milton, Jem: www.jmiltondraws.com, Twitter/Instagram: @jmiltondraws

Mitchell, Saundra: https://saundramitchell.com, Twitter: @SaundraMitchell,
Instagram: @smitchellbooks

Moon, Sarah: https://sarahmoonbooks.com, Twitter: @sarahmoonbooks

Moore, Pamela: www.harpercollins.com/blogs/authors/pamela-moore
-88000054930

Muir, Tamsyn: http://tamsynmuir.com, Twitter: @tazmuir

Muldoon, Molly: www.passingfair.com, Twitter/Instagram: @passingfair

Murray, Sheryl: www.sherylmurray.com, Twitter: @Sheryl_Murray, Instagram:
@sheryl_murray_illustration

Namir, Hasan: www.hasannamir.com, Twitter: @HNamir, Instagram:
@hasan.namir

Neal, DeShanna: Twitter: @Trinsmamabear

Neal, Trinity: www.penguinrandomhouse.com/authors/2196625/trinity-neal

Neilson, Emily: www.emilyneilson.com, Instagram: @emilyeneilson

Newman, Lesléa: https://lesleanewman.com, Twitter: @lesleanewman

Nguyen, Trung Le: www.trungles.com, Twitter/Instagram: @Trungles

Nijkamp, Marieke: www.mariekenijkamp.com/musings, Twitter/Instagram:
@mariekeyn

Nijland, Stern: www.sternnijland.nl

Ormsbee, Kathryn: https://kathrynormsbee.com, Twitter/Instagram: @Kathsby

Oseman, Alice: https://aliceoseman.com, Twitter/Instagram/YouTube:
@AliceOseman

Ostertag, Molly Knox: www.mollyostertag.com, Twitter: @MollyOstertag,
Instagram: @Molly_Ostertag

Pancholy, Maulik: www.maulikpancholy.com, Twitter/Instagram: @Maulik
Pancholy

Papworth, Sarah: https://sarahpapworth.com, Instagram: @sarahpapworth
design, @sarahpapworthart

Parnell, Peter: https://www.simonandschuster.com/authors/Peter-Parnell/
707666

Passchier, Anne/Andy: http://andypasschier.gay/, Instagram: @andyrogyny

Pawis-Steckley, Joshua Mangeshig: www.mangeshig.com, Instagram:
@mangeshig

Pearlman, Robb: www.robbpearlman.com, Twitter: @msmazeppa, Instagram:
@robbpearlman

Peters, Julie Anne: Twitter: @julieannepeters

Phelps, Amy: https://amythystart.weebly.com, Twitter: @amythyst_art,
Instagram: @amythysttt

Pitman, Gayle E.: Twitter: @GaylePitman, Instagram: @pitman_g

Pohl, Laura: https://onlybylaura.com, Twitter/Instagram: @onlybylaura

Polacco, Patricia: http://patriciapolacco.com, Twitter: @PatriciaPolacco,
Instagram: @patriciapolacco001

Polonsky, Ami: www.amipolonsky.com

Prager, Sarah: https://sarahprager.com, Twitter: @Sarah_Prager, Instagram:
@sarahpragerbooks

Quindlen, Kelly: www.kellyquindlen.com, Twitter/Instagram: @kellyquindlen

Ralli, Jessica: www.jessicaralli.com, Instagram: @jessicaearlylit

Reyes, Sonora: www.sonorareyes.com, Twitter: @SonoraReyes, Instagram:
@sonora.reyes

Richardson, Justin: www.simonandschuster.com/authors/Justin-Richard-
son/27409275

Riley, Ronnie: www.mxronnieriley.com, Twitter/Instagram: @MxRonnieRiley

Roehrig, Caleb: http://calebroehrig.com, Twitter: @MikalebRoehrig, Instagram:
@calebroehrig

Romanoff, Zan: https://zanromanoff.com, Twitter/Instagram: @zanopticon

Rosswood, Eric: https://ericrosswood.com, Twitter: @LGBT_Activist,
Instagram: @ericrosswood

Rowell, Rainbow: www.rainbowrowell.com, Twitter/Instagram: @rainbow
rowell

Ruiz, Joy Hwang: www.momisdrawing.com/about, Twitter/Instagram:
@momisdrawing

Russo, Meredith: Instagram: @frothyseawitch

Ryon, Loriel: www.lorielryon.com, Twitter/Instagram: @LorielRyon

Sanchez, Alex: www.alexsanchez.com

Sanders, Rob: http://robsanderswrites.blogspot.com, Twitter: @RobSandersWrite

Santana, Sol: Twitter: @SolSantanaXY

Sass, A. J.: https://sassinsf.com, Twitter/Instagram: @matokah

Schiffer, Miriam B.: https://miriamschiffer.com, Instagram: @miriam.b.schiffer

Schneider, Robyn: www.robynschneider.com, Twitter/Instagram: @robyn schneider

Shrum, Brianna R.: https://brianna-shrum.webnode.page, Twitter: @Brianna Shrum, Instagram: @bchrumby

Silvera, Adam: www.adamsilvera.com, Twitter/Instagram: @AdamSilvera

Silverman, Laura: www.laurasilvermanwrites.com, Twitter/Instagram: @LJSilverman1

Sim, Tara: www.tarasim.com, Twitter: @EachStarAWorld, Instagram: @tarasimauthor

Slater, Dashka: www.dashkaslater.com, Twitter: @DashkaSlater, Instagram: @princessamanita

Smedley, Zack: https://zacksmedleyauthor.com, Twitter/Instagram: @Zack _Smedley

Smoka-Richardson, Rachel: http://rachelsmokarichardson.com, Twitter: @RachelSmoka, Instagram: @mnstitchergirl

Smyth, Ciara: https://ciarasmyth.com, Instagram: @ciaraiswriting

Snider, Brandon T.: www.cootiekid.com, Twitter/Instagram: @Brandon TSnider

Song, Mika: https://mikasongdraws.com, Twitter/Instagram: @mikasongdraws

Spillett, Tasha: https://tashaspillett.com, Twitter: @TashaSpillett, Instagram: @tasha.spillett

Stamper, Phil: https://philstamper.com, Twitter/Instagram/TikTok: @stampepk

Stanley, Stan: www.snakewife.com, Twitter: @Snakewife

Sterling, Isabel: www.isabelsterling.com, Twitter: @IsaSterling, Instagram: @isa_sterling

Stevenson, Robin: https://robinstevenson.com, Twitter: @robin_stevenson, Instagram: @robinstevensonwrites

Stoeve, Ray: https://raystoeve.com, Instagram: @raystoeve

Stowell, Louie: https://louiestowell.com, Twitter: @Louiestowell

Stuart, Scott: https://scottstuart.co, Twitter: @scottcreatess, Instagram: @scottcreates, TikTok: @scott.creates

Tamaki, Mariko: Twitter/Instagram: @marikotamaki

Taylor, Will: www.willtaylorbooks.com, Twitter/Instagram: @InkAndHive

Telgemeier, Raina: https://goraina.com, Twitter/Instagram: @goraina

Thomas, Aiden: www.aiden-thomas.com, Twitter/Instagram, TikTok: @aidenschmaiden

Thomas, Leah: www.bloomsbury.com/us/author/leah-thomas/

Thompson, Lin: https://linthompson.com, Twitter: @lin__thompson

Thor, Rosiee: www.rosieethor.com, Twitter/Instagram: @RosieeThor

Tirado, Melita: www.melitatirado.com, Twitter: @mel_tirado

Tirado, Vincent: www.v-e-tirado.com, Twitter: @v_e_tirado

Tobacco, Violet: www.violettobacco.com, Instagram: @violettobacco, Twitter: @TobaccoViolet

Van Otterloo, Ash: www.ashvanotterloo.com, Twitter: @AshVanOtterloo, Instagram: @ashvanotterloobooks

van Whye, Kevin: www.penguinrandomhouse.com/authors/2201078/kevin-van-whye

Walker, Suzanne: www.suzannewakeenwalker.com, Twitter: @suzusaur

Wang, Jen: www.jenwang.net, Twitter: @alooghobi, Instagram: @wangstragram

Wells, Rebecca Kim: https://rebeccawellswrites.com, Twitter/Instagram: @rebeccawriting

Wexler, Django: https://djangowexler.com, Twitter/Instagram: @DjangoWexler

White, Andrew Joseph: https://andrewjosephwhite.com, Twitter/Instagram: @AJWhiteAuthor, TikTok: @AndrewJosephWhite

Wild, Charlotte Sullivan: https://charlotteswild.com, Twitter: @SullivanWild, Instagram: @charlottesullivanwild

Winters, Julian: Twitter: @julianw_writes, Instagram: @wintersjulian

Wixted, Kristen: www.kristenwixted.com, Twitter/Instagram: @KPWix

Woodfolk, Ashley: www.ashleywoodfolk.com, Twitter/Instagram: @AshWrites

Woodgate, Harry: www.harrywoodgate.com, Twitter: @harryewoodgate, Instagram: @harrywoooodgate

Xu, Wendy: www.artofwendyxu.com

Yang, Gene Luen: https://geneyang.com, Twitter/Instagram: @geneluenyang

Yang, J: https://jyangart.com, Twitter: @artofjyang, Instagram: @wingedkoi

Young, Keezy: www.keezyyoung.com. Twitter: @KeezyBees, Instagram: @keezyyoung

GLOSSARY

ace. *See* ASEXUAL.

agender. A person who does not identify with a gender, feels an absence of gender, or is otherwise genderless.

alloromantic. Someone who experiences romantic attraction to other people.

allosexual. Someone who experiences sexual attraction to other people.

aromantic. Someone who does not experience romantic attraction to other people or who experiences romantic attraction only rarely or under specific circumstances. *See also* DEMIROMANTIC, GRAYROMANTIC, SPLIT ATTRACTION MODEL.

asexual (or ace). Someone who does not experience sexual attraction to other people or who experiences sexual attraction only rarely or under specific circumstances. Asexuality is not the same as celibacy (not having sex) or low or no libido. *See also* DEMISEXUAL, GRAYSEXUAL, SPLIT ATTRACTION MODEL.

bigender. Someone who has two distinct gender identities that can exist at the same time or be fluid or change.

bisexual. Someone who experiences romantic and/or sexual attraction to two or more genders. In general usage, this term is often used to mean being attracted to *both* men and women, but it does not need to refer to a gender binary or *same* and *opposite* gender. *See also* OMNISEXUAL, PANSEXUAL, POLYSEXUAL.

cisgender. Someone whose gender identity aligns with their sex assigned at birth.

demiboy. Someone who partially identifies as a man, boy, male, and/or masculine.

demigirl. Someone who partially identifies as a girl, woman, female, and/or feminine.

demiromantic. Someone who does not feel romantic attraction to someone else unless they have a deep emotional bond with that person first.

demisexual. Someone who does not feel sexual attraction to someone else unless they have a deep emotional bond with that person first.

enby. *See* NONBINARY.

gay. 1: A man who is sexually and/or romantically attracted to other men. *See also* MLM. **2:** As an umbrella term, *gay* can mean anyone who is sexually and/or romantically attracted to other people of the same gender, or any other queer/LGBTQIA+ identities. *See also* QUEER.

gender expression. How someone shows their gender(s) through clothing, hair, or other means.

gender identity. The gender(s) a person feels they are.

gender nonconforming. Someone who does not fit the strict constraints of gender roles or who does not meet expectations for behavior or presentation.

gender perception. How someone's gender identity is perceived by others.

gender performance. How someone expresses their gender(s) based on cultural ideas of gender.

gender-fluid. A gender that varies over time, which could be moment to moment or over the course of years, or anything in between. The variation could be subtle or drastic.

genderqueer. A term that can be used by anyone who has an atypical experience of their gender.

grayromantic. A person who only rarely, or in limited circumstances, experiences romantic attraction to another person.

graysexual. A person who only rarely, or in limited circumstances, experiences sexual attraction to another person.

heterosexual. Someone who experiences sexual and/or romantic attraction to people of a different gender. *See also* STRAIGHT.

homosexual. Someone who experiences sexual and/or romantic attraction to people of their same gender.

intersex. An umbrella term for a group of conditions that leads to someone being born with reproductive or sexual anatomy or chromosomal patterns that don't fit typical or specific definitions of male or female. This could mean *ambiguous genitalia,* internal reproductive organs/anatomy that do not typically match the external reproductive organs/anatomy, or chromosomal variations.

lesbian. Women who are sexually and/or romantically attracted to other women, though the term can also be used by some nonbinary people. *See also* HOMOSEXUAL, SAPPHIC, WLW.

microlabels. Specific descriptors of a person's experience with gender, romantic attraction, and/or sexual attraction, usually falling under the umbrella terms of *transgender, aromantic,* or *asexual.* An example is *quoisexual,* or someone who is unsure of what sexual attraction is or feels like or is unsure if they experience sexual attraction. *See also* SPLIT ATTRACTION MODEL.

MLM: Men who love men. *See also* GAY, HOMOSEXUAL.

nonbinary (*or* enby). An umbrella term for any person who does not identify or is not on a binary male/female spectrum. Nonbinary people may or may not identify as transgender. *See also* AGENDER, BIGENDER, DEMIBOY, DEMIGIRL, GENDER NONCONFORMING, GENDER-FLUID, GENDERQUEER, OMNIGENDER, PANGENDER, POLYGENDER, TWO SPIRIT.

omnigender. Someone who experiences almost every gender, but not quite, or someone who experiences all genders but treats them all as one. *See also* PANGENDER.

omnisexual. Someone who feels or can feel sexual attraction to all genders.

pangender. A gender identity describing a person who has multiple and infinite genders that may or may not shift over time.

pansexual. Someone whose romantic and/or sexual attraction to someone else does not depend on the other person's gender.

polyamory. A relationship involving more than two people. Someone who is *polyamorous* has more than one partner at a time.

polygender. Someone who experiences more than one gender.

polysexual. Someone who is sexually attracted to multiple genders, but not necessarily all.

queer. Any identity that is not STRAIGHT/HETEROSEXUAL, CISGENDER, ALLOSEXUAL, and ALLOROMANTIC.

queerplatonic relationship. A committed relationship that is somewhere beyond or different from friendship, but not romantic or sexual.

questioning. Anyone who is unsure of their sexual, gender, or romantic identity.

romantic orientation. The circumstances in which someone feels romantic attraction to other people.

sapphic. A woman who is attracted to other women, regardless of orientation or labels.

sexual orientation. The circumstances in which someone feels sexual attraction to other people.

split attraction model. For most people, sexual attraction and romantic attraction line up neatly. Not everyone is like that, though, especially those people under the *asexual* and/or *aromantic* umbrellas. Any of the sexual orientation prefixes can be used with the romantic suffix (e.g., *biromantic, heteroromantic, demiromantic*).

straight. A person who is romantically and/or sexually attracted to people of a different gender. *See also* HETEROSEXUAL.

transgender. Someone who does not identify with the gender they were assigned at birth and/or someone who identifies with a gender other than that which they were assigned at birth. *See also* NONBINARY.

two spirit. This term is very specific to people in Indigenous, First Nations, and Native American communities. People who are not part of an Indigenous, a First Nations, or a Native American community should not use this term. It refers to a person who has both a masculine and a feminine spirit. This can encompass sexual, romantic, gender, and/or spiritual identity, as well as gender expression and gender roles.

WLW. Women who love women. *See also* LESBIAN, SAPPHIC.

ABOUT THE AUTHORS
AND CONTRIBUTORS

Kathleen Breitenbach (they/them) has been the Teen Librarian at the Hamilton Township (NJ) Public Library since 2009 and is the 2022–2023 past chair of the Rainbow Round Table. They have served for two years on the Rainbow Book List Committee (once as co-chair, 2017; once as chair, 2020) and two years on the Stonewall Book Awards–Mike Morgan and Larry Romans Children's and Young Adult Literature Committee (2018; chair 2019) for the Rainbow Round Table; chaired Popular Paperbacks for Young Adults (2017) for YALSA; and spoken on LGBTQIA+ issues and youth literature in webinars and conference programs.

Liz Deskins was a school librarian for thirty years, teaching at the elementary, high school, and college levels. Now retired, she is an adjunct professor for Kent State University. Liz has served on committees and task forces for the American Association of School Librarians and the Association for Library Service to Children. Liz also sat on the Stonewall Book Awards–Mike Morgan and Larry Romans Children's and Young Adult Literature Committee with Kathleen Breitenbach. Her publications include *Linking Picture Book Biographies to National Content Standards: 200+ Lives to Explore* (Libraries Unlimited, 2015); *LGBTQAI+ Books for Children and Teens: Providing a Window for All* (ALA Editions, 2018), coauthored with Christina Dorr; and *Content-Area Collaborations for Secondary Grades* (ALA Editions, 2019).

Kit Ballenger: Executive director, Pride and Less Prejudice

Katy Hume: Marketing, Book Retail

Meaghan Hummel: Social studies teacher, sixth grade, Parker Junior High, Flossmoor, IL

Ariana Hussain: Teacher librarian, Blake School, Minneapolis, MN

Noah D. Mullens: PhD student, University of Florida, Gainesville, FL

Shira Pilarski: Assistant manager, Detroit Public Library, MI

Dave Saia: Librarian, Heim Middle School, Williamsville, NY

Kelly Silwani: School librarian, Orange Middle School, Lewis Center, OH

Allie Stevens: Director, Calhoun County Library and Museum, Hampton, AR

Tiffany Thomas: Librarian, Hilliard Bradley High School, Hilliard, OH

Jessica Williams: Graduate student, Kent State University, Kent, OH

AUTHOR/TITLE INDEX

SUBJECT INDEX

You may also be interested in . . .

ISBN: 978-0-8389-9485-6

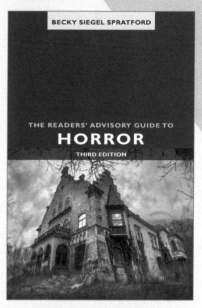

ISBN: 978-0-8389-4876-7

ISBN: 978-0-8389-4747-0

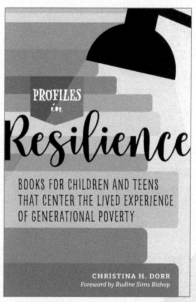

ISBN: 978-0-8389-3788-4

For more titles, visit **alastore.ala.org**